HANDBOOK OF SOIL SCIENCE

HANDBOOK OF SOIL SCIENCE

By

Dr. Shubhrata R. Mishra
Deptt. of Botany
Vikram University
Ujjain (M.P.)
(India)

DPH

DISCOVERY PUBLISHING HOUSE PVT. LTD.
NEW DELHI-110 002

Published by:
Tilak Wasan

DISCOVERY PUBLISHING HOUSE PVT. LTD.
4383/4A, Ansari Road, Darya Ganj
New Delhi-110 002 (India)
Phone : +91-11-23279245, 43596064-65
Fax : +91-11-23253475
E-mail : parul.wasan@gmail.com
discoverypublishinghouse@gmail.com
web : www.discoverypublishinggroup.com

***First Edition:* 2012**
ISBN: 978-93-5056-005-1

Handbook of Soil Science

Printed at:
Shree Balaji Art Press
Delhi

Preface

Soil science is the study of soil as a natural resource on the surface of the earth including soil formation, classification and mapping; physical, chemical, biological, and fertility properties of soils; and these properties in relation to the use and management of soils.

Sometimes terms which refer to branches of soil science, such as pedology (formation, chemistry, morphology and classification of soil) and edaphology (influence of soil on organisms, especially plants), are used as if synonymous with soil science. The diversity of names associated with this discipline is related to the various associations concerned. Indeed, engineers, agronomists, chemists, geologists, geographers, ecologists, biologists, microbiologists, sylviculturists, sanitarians, archaeologists, and specialists in regional planning, all contribute to further knowledge of soils and the advancement of the soil sciences.

Soil is a natural body consisting of layers (soil horizons) of mineral constituents of variable thicknesses, which differ from the parent materials in their morphological, physical, chemical, and mineralogical characteristics.

It is composed of particles of broken rock that have been altered by chemical and environmental processes that include weathering and erosion. Soil differs from its parent rock due to interactions between the lithosphere, hydrosphere, atmosphere, and the biosphere. It is a mixture of mineral and organic constituents that are in solid, gaseous and aqueous states. Soil particles pack loosely, forming a soil structure filled with pore spaces. These pores contain soil solution (liquid) and air (gas). Accordingly, soils are often treated as a three state-system.

Most soils have a density between 1 and 2 g/cm^3. Soil is also known as earth: it is the substance from which our planet takes its name. Little of the soil composition of planet Earth is older than the Tertiary and most no older than the Pleistocene. In engineering, soil is referred to as regolith, or loose rock material.

Soil occupies the pedosphere, one of Earth's spheres that the geosciences use to organize the Earth conceptually. This is the conceptual perspective of pedology and edaphology, the two main branches of soil science. Pedology is the study of soil in its natural setting. Edaphology is the study of soil in relation to soil-dependent uses. Both branches apply a combination of soil physics, soil chemistry, and soil biology. Due to the numerous interactions between the biosphere, atmosphere and hydrosphere that are hosted within the pedosphere, more integrated, less soil-centric concepts are also valuable. Many concepts essential to understanding soil come from individuals not identifiable strictly as soil scientists. This highlights the interdisciplinary nature of soil concepts.

Author

Contents

1 Introduction

Soil science is the study of soil as a natural resource on the surface of the earth including soil formation, classification and mapping; physical, chemical, biological, and fertility properties of soils; and these properties in relation to the use and management of soils.

Sometimes terms which refer to branches of soil science, such as pedology (formation, chemistry, morphology and classification of soil) and edaphology (influence of soil on organisms, especially plants), are used as if synonymous with soil science. The diversity of names associated with this discipline is related to the various associations concerned. Indeed, engineers, agronomists, chemists, geologists, geographers, ecologists, biologists, microbiologists, sylviculturists, sanitarians, archaeologists, and specialists in regional planning, all contribute to further knowledge of soils and the advancement of the soil sciences.

Fields of Study

Soil occupies the pedosphere, one of Earth's spheres that the geosciences use to organize the Earth conceptually. This is the conceptual perspective of pedology and edaphology, the two main branches of soil science. Pedology is the study of soil in its natural setting. Edaphology is the study of soil in relation to soil-dependent uses. Both branches apply a combination of soil physics, soil chemistry, and soil biology. Due to the numerous interactions between the biosphere, atmosphere and hydrosphere that are hosted within the pedosphere, more integrated, less soil-centric concepts are also valuable. Many concepts essential to understanding soil come from individuals not identifiable strictly as soil scientists. This highlights the interdisciplinary nature of soil concepts.

Research

Dependence on and curiosity about soil, exploring the diversity and dynamic of this resource continues to yield fresh discoveries and insights. New avenues of soil research are compelled by a need to understand soil in the context of climate change greenhouse gases, and carbon sequestration, interest in maintaining the planet's biodiversity and in exploring past cultures has also stimulated renewed interest in achieving a more refined understanding of soil.

Mapping

Most empirical knowledge of soil in nature comes from soil survey efforts. Soil survey, or soil mapping, is the process of determining the soil types or other properties of the soil cover over a landscape, and mapping them for others to understand and use. It relies heavily on distinguishing the individual influences of the five classic soil forming factors. This effort draws upon geomorphology, physical geography, and analysis of vegetation and land-use patterns. Primary data for the soil survey are acquired by field sampling and supported by remote sensing.

Classification

As of 2006, the World Reference Base for Soil Resources, via its Land and Water Development division, is the pre-eminent soil classification system. It replaces the previous FAO soil classification.

The WRB borrows from modern soil classification concepts, including USDA soil taxonomy. The classification is based mainly on soil morphology as an expression pedogenesis. A major difference with USDA soil taxonomy is that soil climate is not part of the system, except insofar as climate influences soil profile characteristics.

Many other classification schemes exist, including vernacular systems. The structure in vernacular systems are either nominal, giving unique names to soils or landscapes, or descriptive, naming soils by their characteristics such as red, hot, fat, or sandy. Soils are distinguished by obvious characteristics, such as physical appearance (e.g., colour, texture, landscape position), performance (e.g., production capability, flooding), and accompanying vegetation. A vernacular distinction familiar to many is classifying texture as heavy or light. Light soil content and better structure, take less effort to turn and cultivate. Contrary to popular belief, light soils do not weigh less than heavy soils on an air dry basis nor do they have more porosity.

History

Vasily Dokuchaev, a Russian geologist, geographer and early soil scientist, is credited with identifying soil as a resource whose distinctness and complexity deserved to be separated conceptually from geology and crop production and treated as a whole.

Previously, soil had been considered a product of chemical transformations of rocks, a dead substrate from which plants derive nutritious elements. Soil and bedrock were in fact equated. Dokuchaev considers the soil as a natural body having its own genesis and its own history of development, a body with complex and multiform processes taking place within it. The soil is considered as different from bedrock. The latter becomes soil under the influence of a series of soil-formation factors (climate, vegetation, country, relief and age). According to him, soil should be called the 'daily' or outward horizons of rocks regardless of the type; they are changed naturally by the common effect of water, air and various kinds of living and dead organisms.

A 1914 encyclopedic definition: 'the different forms of earth on the surface of the rocks, formed by the breaking down or weathering of rocks' serves to illustrate the historic view of soil which persisted from the 19th century. Dokuchaev's late 19th century soil concept developed in the 20th century to one of soil as earthy material that has been altered by living processes. A corollary concept is that soil without a living component is simply a part of earth's outer layer.

Further refinement of the soil concept is occurring in view of an appreciation of energy transport and transformation within soil. The term is popularly applied to the material on the surface of the earth's moon and Mars, a usage acceptable within a portion of the scientific community. Accurate to this modern understanding of soil is Nikiforoff's 1959 definition of soil as the 'excited skin of the sub aerial part of the earth's crust'.

Areas of Practice

Academically, soil scientists tend to be drawn to one of five areas of specialization: microbiology, pedology, edaphology, physics or chemistry. Yet the work specifics are very much dictated by the challenges facing our civilization's desire to sustain the land that supports it, and the distinctions between the sub-disciplines of soil science often blur in the process. Soil science professionals commonly stay current in soil chemistry, soil physics, soil microbiology, pedology, and applied soil science in related disciplines.

One interesting effort drawing in soil scientists in the USA as of 2004 is the Soil Quality Initiative. Central to the Soil Quality Initiative is developing indices of soil health and then monitoring them in a way that gives us long term (decade-to-decade) feedback on our performance as stewards of the planet. The effort includes understanding the functions of soil microbiotic crusts and exploring the potential to sequester atmospheric carbon in soil organic matter. The concept of soil quality, however, has not been without its share of controversy and criticism, including critiques by Nobel Laureate Norman Borlaug and World Food Prize Winner Pedro Sanchez.

A more traditional role for soil scientists has been to map soils. Most every area in the United States now has a published soil survey, which includes interpretive tables as to how soil properties support or limit activities and uses. An internationally accepted soil taxonomy allows uniform communication of soil characteristics and functions. National and international soil survey efforts have given the profession unique insights into landscape scale functions. The landscape functions that soil scientists are called upon to address in the field seem to fall roughly into six areas:

Land-based Treatment of Wastes

- Septic system
- Manure
- Municipal biosolids
- Food and fiber processing waste

Identification and Protection of Environmentally Critical Areas

- Sensitive and unstable soils
- Wetlands
- Unique soil situations that support valuable habitat, and ecosystem diversity

Management for Optimum Land Productivity

- Silviculture
- Agronomy
- Nutrient management

- Water management
- Native vegetation
- Grazing

Management for Optimum Water Quality

- Stormwater management
- Sediment and erosion control

Remediation and Restoration of Damaged Lands

- Mine reclamation
- Flood and storm damage
- Contamination

Sustainability of Desired Uses

There are also practical applications of soil science that might not be apparent from looking at a published soil survey.

Radiometric dating: specifically a knowledge of local pedology is used to date prior activity at the site.

Stratification (archaeology) where soil formation processes and preservative qualities can inform the study of archaeological sites.

- Geological Phenomena
- Landslides
- Earthquakes faults

Altering Soils to Achieve New Uses

Vitrification to contain radioactive wastes

Enhancing soil microbial capabilities in degrading contaminants bioremediation).

Carbon Sequestration

- Environmental soil science
- Pedology

- Soil genesis
- Pedometrics
- Soil morphology
- Soil micromorphology
- Soil classification
- USDA soil taxonomy
- Soil biology
- Soil microbiology
- Soil chemistry
- Soil biochemistry
- Soil mineralogy
- Soil physics

Pedotransfer Function

- Soil mechanics and engineering
- Soil hydrology, hydropedology

Fields of Application in Soil Science

- Soil survey
- Soil management
- Standard methods of analysis
- Soil fertility/Nutrient management
- Ecosystem studies
- Climate change
- Watershed and wetland studies
- Pedotransfer function

Related Disciplines

- Agricultural sciences
- Agrophysics science
- Irrigation management

- Anthropology
- archaeological stratigraphy

Environmental Science

- Landscape ecology
- Geography
- Physical geography
- Geology
- Biogeochemistry
- Geomicrobiology
- Geomorphology
- Hydrology
- Hydrogeology
- Waste management
- Wetland science

2 Soil

Soil is a natural body consisting of layers (soil horizons) of mineral constituents of variable thicknesses, which differ from the parent materials in their morphological, physical, chemical, and mineralogical characteristics.

It is composed of particles of broken rock that have been altered by chemical and environmental processes that include weathering and erosion. Soil differs from its parent rock due to interactions between the lithosphere, hydrosphere, atmosphere, and the biosphere. It is a mixture of mineral and organic constituents that are in solid, gaseous and aqueous states. Soil particles pack loosely, forming a soil structure filled with pore spaces. These pores contain soil solution (liquid) and air (gas). Accordingly, soils are often treated as a three state-system.

Most soils have a density between 1 and 2 g/cm^3. Soil is also known as earth: it is the substance from which our planet takes its name. Little of the soil composition of planet Earth is older than the Tertiary and most no older than the Pleistocene. In engineering, soil is referred to as regolith, or loose rock material.

Soil Forming Factors

Soil formation, or pedogenesis, is the combined effect of physical, chemical, biological, and anthropogenic processes on soil parent material. Soil genesis involves processes that develop layers or horizons in the soil profile. These processes involve additions, losses, transformations and translocations of material that compose the soil. Minerals derived from weathered rocks undergo changes that cause the formation of secondary minerals and other compounds that are variably soluble in water, these constituents are moved (translocated) from one area of the soil to other areas by water and animal activity. The alteration and movement of materials within soil causes the formation of distinctive soil horizons.

The weathering of bedrock produces the parent material from which soils form. An example of soil development from bare rock occurs on recent lava flows in warm regions under heavy and very frequent rainfall. In such climates, plants become established very quickly on basaltic lava, even though there is very little organic material. The plants are supported by the porous rock as it is filled with nutrient-bearing water which carries, for example, dissolved minerals and guano. The developing plant roots, themselves or associated with mycorrhizal fungi, gradually break up the porous lava and organic matter soon accumulates.

But even before it does, the predominantly porous broken lava in which the plant roots grow can be considered a soil. How the soil 'life' cycle proceeds is influenced by at least five classic soil forming factors that are dynamically intertwined in shaping the way soil is developed, they include: parent material, regional climate, topography, biotic potential and the passage of time.

Parent Material

The material from which soils form is called parent material. It includes: weathered primary bedrock; secondary material transported from other locations, e.g. colluvium and alluvium; deposits that are already present but mixed or altered in other ways — old soil formations, organic material including peat or alpine humus; and anthropogenic materials, like landfill or mine waste. Few soils form directly from the breakdown of the underlying rocks they develop on. These soils are often called 'residual soils', and have the same general chemistry as their parent rocks. Most soils derive from materials that have been transported from other locations by wind, water and gravity. Some of these materials may have moved many miles or only a few feet. Windblown material called loess is common in the Midwest of North America and in Central Asia and other locations. Glacial till is a component of many soils in the northern and southern latitudes and those formed near large mountains; till is the product of glacial ice moving over the ground. The ice can break rock and larger stones into smaller pieces, it also can sort material into different sizes. As glacial ice melts, the melt water also moves and sorts material, and deposits it varying distances from its origin. The deeper sections of the soil profile may have materials that are relatively unchanged from when they were deposited by water, ice or wind.

Weather is the first stage in the transforming of parent material into soil material. In soils forming from bedrock, a thick layer of weathered material called saprolite may form. Saprolite is the result of weathering processes that include: hydrolysis (the replacement of a mineral's cations with hydrogen ions), chelation from organic compounds, hydration (the absorption of water by minerals), solution of minerals by water, and physical processes that include freezing and thawing or wetting and drying. The mineralogical and chemical composition of the primary bedrock material, plus physical features, including grain size and degree of consolidation, plus the rate and type of weathering, transforms it into different soil materials.

Climate

Soil formation greatly depends on the climate, and soils from different climate zones show distinctive characteristics. Temperature and moisture affect weathering and leaching. Wind moves sand and other particles, especially in arid regions where there is little plant cover. The type and amount of precipitation influence soil formation by affecting the movement of ions and particles through the soil, aiding in the development of different soil profiles. Seasonal and daily temperature fluctuations affect the effectiveness of water in weathering parent rock material and affect soil dynamics. The cycle of freezing and thawing is an effective mechanism to break up rocks and other consolidated materials. Temperature and precipitation rates affect biological activity, rates of chemical reactions and types of vegetation cover.

Biological Factors

Plants, animals, fungi, bacteria and humans affect soil formation. Animals and micro-organisms mix soils to form burrows and pores allowing moisture and gases to seep into deeper layers. In the same way, plant roots open channels in the soils, especially plants with deep taproots which can penetrate many meters through the different soil layers to bring up nutrients from deeper in the soil. Plants with fibrous roots that spread out near the soil surface, have roots that are easily decomposed, adding organic matter. Micro-organisms, including fungi and bacteria, affect chemical exchanges between roots and soil and act as a reserve of nutrients. Humans can impact soil formation by removing vegetation cover; this removal promotes erosion. They can also mix the different soil layers, restarting the soil formation process as less-weathered material is mixed with and diluting the more developed upper layers.

Vegetation impacts soils in numerous ways. It can prevent erosion from rain or surface runoff. It shades soils, keeping them cooler and slowing evaporation of soil moisture, or it can cause soils to dry out by transpiration. Plants can form new chemicals that break down or build up soil particles. Vegetation depends on climate, land form topography and biological factors. Soil factors such as soil density, depth, chemistry, pH, temperature and moisture greatly affect the type of plants that can grow in a given location. Dead plants, dropped leaves and stems of plants fall to the surface of the soil and decompose. There, organisms feed on them and mix the organic material with the upper soil layers; these organic compounds become part of the soil formation process, ultimately shaping the type of soil formed.

Time is a factor in the interactions of all the above factors as they develop soil. Over time, soils evolve features dependent on the other forming factors, and soil formation is a time-responsive process dependent on how the other factors interplay with each other. Soil is always changing. For example, recently-deposited material from a flood exhibits no soil development because there has not been enough time for soil-forming activities. The soil surface is buried, and the formation process begins again for this soil. The long periods over which change occurs and its multiple influences mean that simple soils are rare, resulting in the formation of soil horizons. While soil can achieve relative stability in properties for extended periods, the soil life cycle ultimately ends in soil conditions that leave it vulnerable to erosion. Despite the inevitability of soil retrogression and degradation, most soil cycles are long and productive.

Soil-forming factors continue to affect soils during their existence, even on 'stable' landscapes that are long-enduring, some for millions of years. Materials are deposited on top and materials are blown or washed away from the surface. With additions, removals and alterations, soils are always subject to new conditions. Whether these are slow or rapid changes depend on climate, landscape position and biological activity.

Characteristics

Striking colours and contrasting patterns are especially memorable and it is often the first impression one has when viewing soil. The Red River (Mississippi watershed) carries sediment eroded from extensive reddish soils like Port Silt Loam in Oklahoma. The Yellow River in China carries yellow sediment from eroding loessal soils. Mollisols in the Great Plains are darkened and enriched by organic matter. Podsols in boreal forests have highly contrasting layers due to acidity and leaching. Soil colour is primarily influenced by soil mineralogy. Many soil colours are due to the extensive and various iron minerals. The development and distribution of colour in a soil profile result from chemical and biological weathering, especially redox reactions. As the primary minerals in soil parent material weather, the elements combine into new and colourful compounds. Iron forms secondary minerals with a yellow or red colour, organic matter decomposes into black and brown compounds, and manganese, sulfur and nitrogen can form black mineral deposits. These pigments produce various colour patterns due to effects by the environment during soil formation. Aerobic conditions produce uniform or gradual colour changes, while reducing environments result in disrupted colour flow with complex, mottled patterns and points of colour concentration.

Soil structure is the arrangement of soil particles into aggregates. These may have various shapes, sizes and degrees of development or expression. Soil structure affects aeration, water movement, resistance to erosion and plant root growth. Structure often gives clues to texture, organic matter content, biological activity, past soil evolution, human use, and chemical and mineralogical conditions under which the soil formed.

Soil texture refers to sand, silt and clay composition. Soil content affects soil behaviour, including the retention capacity for nutrients and water. Sand and silt are the products of physical weathering, while clay is the product of chemical weathering. Clay content has retention capacity for nutrients and water. Clay soils resist wind and water erosion better than silty and sandy soils, because the particles are more tightly joined to each other. In medium-textured soils, clay is often translocated downward through the soil profile and accumulates in the subsoil.

The electrical resistivity of soil can affect the rate of galvanic corrosion of metallic structures in contact with the soil. Higher moisture content or increased electrolyte concentration can lower the resistivity and thereby increase the rate of corrosion. Soil resistivity values typically range from about 2 to 1000 Ω·m, but more extreme values are not unusual.

Soil Horizons

The naming of soil horizons is based on the type of material the horizons are composed of; these materials reflect the duration of the specific processes used in soil formation. They are labelled using a short hand notation of letters and numbers. They are described and classified by their colour, size, texture, structure, consistency, root quantity, pH, voids, boundary characteristics, and if they have nodules or concretions. Any one soil profile does not have all the major horizons covered below; soils may have few or many horizons.

The exposure of parent material to favorable conditions produces initial soils that are suitable for plant growth. Plant growth often results in the accumulation of organic residues, the accumulated organic layer is called the O horizon. Biological organisms colonize and break down organic materials, making available nutrients that other plants and animals can live on. After sufficient time a distinctive organic surface layer forms with humus which is called the A horizon.

Classification

Soil is classified into categories in order to understand relationships between different soils and to determine the usefulness of a soil for a particular use. One of the first classification systems was developed by the Russian scientist Dokuchaev around 1880. It was modified a number of times by American and European researchers, and developed into the system commonly used until the 1960s. It was based on the idea that soils have a particular morphology based on the materials and factors that form them. In the 1960s, a different classification system began to emerge, that focussed on soil morphology instead of parental materials and soil-forming factors. Since then it has undergone further modifications. The World Reference Base for Soil Resources (WRB) aims to establish an international reference base for soil classification.

Orders

Orders are the highest category of soil classification. Order types end in the letters sol. In the US classification system, there are 10 orders:

- *Entisol* — recently formed soils that lack well-developed horizons. Commonly found on unconsolidated sediments like sand, some have an A horizon on top of bedrock.
- *Vertisol* — inverted soils. They tend to swell when wet and shrink upon drying, often forming deep cracks that surface layers can fall into.
- *Inceptisol* — young soils. They have subsurface horizon formation but show little eluviation and illuviation.
- *Aridisol* — dry soils forming under desert conditions. They include nearly 20 per cent of soils on Earth. Soil formation is slow, and accumulated organic matter is scarce. They may have subsurface zones (calcic horizons) where calcium carbonates have accumulated from percolating water. Many aridiso soils have well-developed Bt horizons showing clay movement from past periods of greater moisture.
- *Mollisol* — soft soils with very thick A horizons.
- *Spodosol* — soils produced by podsolization. They are typical soils of coniferous and deciduous forests in cooler climates.

- *Alfisol* — soils with aluminium and iron. They have horizons of clay accumulation, and form where there is enough moisture and warmth for at least three months of plant growth.
- *Ultisol* — soils that are heavily leached.
- *Oxisol* — soil with heavy oxide content.
- *Histosol* — organic soils.

Other order schemes may include:

- *Andisols* — volcanic soils, which tend to be high in glass content.
- *Gelisols* — permafrost soils.

Organic Matter

Most living things in soils, including plants, insects, bacteria and fungi, are dependent on organic matter for nutrients and energy. Soils often have varying degrees of organic compounds in different states of decomposition. Many soils, including desert and rocky-gravel soils, have no or little organic matter. Soils that are all organic matter, such as peat (histosols), are infertile.

Humus

Humus refers to organic matter that has decomposed to a point where it is resistant to further breakdown or alteration. Humic acids and fulvic acids are important constituents of humus and typically form from plant residues like foliage, stems and roots. After death, these plant residues begin to decay, starting the formation of humus. Humus formation involves changes within the soil and plant residue, there is a reduction of water soluble constituents including cellulose and hemicellulose; as the residues are deposited and break down, humin, lignin and lignin complexes accumulate within the soil; as microorganisms live and feed on the decaying plant matter, an increase in proteins occurs.

Lignin is resistant to breakdown and accumulates within the soil; it also chemically reacts with amino acids which add to its resistance to decomposition, including enzymatic decomposition by microbes. Fats and waxes from plant matter have some resistance to decomposition and persist in soils for a while. Clay soils often have higher organic contents that persist longer than soils without clay. Proteins normally decompose readily, but when bound to clay particles they become more resistant to decomposition. Clay particles also absorb enzymes that would break down proteins. The addition of organic matter to clay soils, can render the organic matter and any added nutrients inaccessible to plants and microbes for many years, since they can bind strongly to the clay. High soil tannin (polyphenol) content from plants can cause nitrogen to be sequestered by proteins or cause nitrogen immobilization, also making nitrogen unavailable to plants.

Humus formation is a process dependent on the amount of plant material added each year and the type of base soil; both are affected by climate and the type of organisms present. Soils with humus can vary in nitrogen content but have 3 to 6 per cent nitrogen typically; humus, as a reserve of nitrogen and phosphorus, is a vital component affecting soil fertility. Humus also absorbs water, acting as a moisture reserve, that plants can utilize; it also expands and shrinks between dry and wet states, providing pore spaces. Humus is less stable than other soil constituents, because it is affected by microbial decomposition, and over time its concentration decreases without the addition of new organic matter. However, some forms of humus are highly stable and may persist over centuries if not millennia: they are issued from the slow oxidation of charcoal, also called black carbon, like in Amazonian Terra preta or Black Earths, or from the sequestration of humic compounds within mineral horizons, like in podzols.

Climate and Organics

The production and accumulation or degradation of organic matter and humus is greatly dependent on climate conditions. Temperature and soil moisture are the major factors in the formation or degradation of organic matter, they along with topography, determine the formation of organic soils. Soils high in organic matter tend to form under wet or cold conditions where decomposer activity is impeded by low temperature or excess moisture.

Soil Solutions

Different soils, under varying conditions, have diverse colloidal solutions. These solutions exchange gases with the soil atmosphere. These solutions can contain dissolved sugars; fulvic acids and other organic acids; plant micronutrients such as zinc, iron and copper, plus other metals; ammonium plus a host of others. Some soils have sodium solutions that greatly impact plant growth, calcium is common in forest soils. Soil pH effects the type and amount of anions and cations that soil solutions contain and exchange with the soil atmosphere and biological organisms.

In Nature

Biogeography is the study of special variations in biological communities. Soils are a restricting factor as to which plants can grow in which environments. Soil scientists survey soils in the hope of understanding controls as to what vegetation can and will grow in a particular location.

Geologists also have a particular interest in the patterns of soil on the surface of the earth. Soil texture, colour and chemistry often reflect the underlying geologic parent material, and soil types often change at geologic unit boundaries. Buried paleosols mark previous land surfaces and record climatic conditions from previous eras. Geologists use this paleopedological record to understand the ecological relationships in past ecosystems. According to the theory of biorhexistasy, prolonged conditions conducive to forming deep, weathered soils result in increasing ocean salinity and the formation of limestone.

Geologists use soil profile features to establish the duration of surface stability in the context of geologic faults or slope stability. An offset subsoil horizon indicates rupture during soil formation and the degree of subsequent subsoil formation is relied upon to establish time since rupture.

Soil examined in shovel test pits is used by archaeologists for relative dating based on stratigraphy (as opposed to absolute dating). What is considered most typical is to use soil profile features to determine the maximum reasonable pit depth than needs to be examined for archaeological evidence in the interest of cultural resources management.

Soils altered or formed by man (anthropic and anthropogenic soils) are also of interest to archaeologists, such as terra preta soils.

Soil is used in agriculture, where it serves as the primary nutrient base for plants; however, as demonstrated by hydroponics, it is not essential to plant growth if the soil-contained nutrients could be dissolved in a solution. The types of soil used in agriculture (among other things, such as the purported level of moisture in the soil) vary with respect to the species of plants that are cultivated.

Soil material is a critical component in the mining and construction industries. Soil serves as a foundation for most construction projects. Massive volumes of soil can be involved in surface mining, road building and dam construction. Earth sheltering is the architectural practice of using soil for external thermal mass against building walls.

Soil resources are critical to the environment, as well as to food and fiber production. Soil provides minerals and water to plants. Soil absorbs rainwater and releases it later, thus preventing floods and drought. Soil cleans the water as it percolates. Soil is the habitat for many organisms: the major part of known and unknown biodiversity is in the soil, in the form of invertebrates (earthworms, woodlice, millipedes, centipedes, snails, slugs, mites, springtails, enchytraeids, nematodes, protists), bacteria, archaea, fungi and algae; and most organisms living above ground have part of them (plants) or spend part of their life cycle (insects) below-ground. Above-ground and below-ground biodiversities are tightly interconnected, making soil protection of paramount importance for any restoration or conservation plan.

Waste management often has a soil component. Septic drain fields treat septic tank effluent using aerobic soil processes. Landfills use soil for daily cover.

Organic soils, especially peat, serve as a significant fuel resource; but wide areas of peat production, such as sphagnum bogs, are now protected because of patrimonial interest.

Both animals and humans in many cultures occasionally consume soil. It has been shown that some monkeys consume soil, together with their preferred food (tree foliage and fruits), in order to alleviate tannin toxicity.

Soils filter and purify water and affect its chemistry. Rain water and pooled water from ponds, lakes and rivers percolate through the soil horizons and the upper rock strata; thus becoming groundwater. Pests (viruses) and pollutants, such as persistent organic pollutants (chlorinated pesticides, PCBs), oils (hydrocarbons), heavy metals (lead, zinc, cadmium), and excess nutrients (nitrates, sulfates, phosphates) are filtered out by the soil . Soil organisms metabolize them or immobilize them in their biomass and necromass, thereby incorporating them into stable humus. The physical integrity of soil is also a prerequisite for avoiding landslides in rugged landscapes.

Degradation

Land degradation is a human-induced or natural process which impairs the capacity of land to function. Soils are the critical component in land degradation when it involves acidification, contamination, desertification, erosion or salination.

While soil acidification of alkaline soils is beneficial, it degrades land when soil acidity lowers crop productivity and increases soil vulnerability to contamination and erosion. Soils are often initially acid because their parent materials were acid and initially low in the basic cations (calcium, magnesium, potassium and sodium). Acidification occurs when these elements are removed from the soil profile by normal rainfall, or the harvesting of forest or agricultural crops. Soil acidification is accelerated by the use of acid-forming nitrogenous fertilizers and by the effects of acid precipitation.

Soil contamination at low levels is often within soil capacity to treat and assimilate. Many waste treatment processes rely on this treatment capacity. Exceeding treatment capacity can damage soil biota and limit soil function. Derelict soils occur where industrial contamination or other development activity damages the soil to such a degree that the land cannot be used safely or productively. Remediation of derelict soil uses principles of geology, physics, chemistry and biology to degrade, attenuate, isolate or remove soil contaminants to restore soil functions and values. Techniques include leaching, air sparging, chemical amendments, phytoremediation, bioremediation and natural attenuation.

Desertification is an environmental process of ecosystem degradation in arid and semi-arid regions, often caused by human activity. It is a common misconception that droughts cause desertification. Droughts are common in arid and semiarid lands. Well-managed lands can recover from drought when the rains return. Soil management tools include maintaining soil nutrient and organic matter levels, reduced tillage and increased cover. These practices help to control erosion and maintain productivity during periods when moisture is available. Continued land abuse during droughts, however, increases land degradation. Increased population and livestock pressure on marginal lands accelerates desertification.

Soil erosional loss is caused by wind, water, ice and movement in response to gravity. Although the processes may be simultaneous, erosion is distinguished from weathering. Erosion is an intrinsic natural process, but in many places it is increased by human land use. Poor land use practices including deforestation, overgrazing and improper construction activity. Improved management can limit erosion by using techniques like limiting disturbance during construction, avoiding construction during erosion prone periods, intercepting runoff, terrace-building, use of erosion-suppressing cover materials, and planting trees or other soil binding plants.

A serious and long-running water erosion problem occurs in China, on the middle reaches of the Yellow River and the upper reaches of the Yangtze River. From the Yellow River, over 1.6-billion tons of sediment flow each year into the ocean. The sediment originates primarily from water erosion (gully erosion) in the Loess Plateau region of northwest China.

Soil piping is a particular form of soil erosion that occurs below the soil surface. It is associated with levee and dam failure, as well as sink hole formation. Turbulent flow removes soil starting from the mouth of the seep flow and subsoil erosion advances upgradient. The term sand boil is used to describe the appearance of the discharging end of an active soil pipe.

Soil salination is the accumulation of free salts to such an extent that it leads to degradation of soils and vegetation. Consequences include corrosion damage, reduced plant growth, erosion due to loss of plant cover and soil structure, and water quality problems due to sedimentation. Salination occurs due to a combination of natural and human caused processes. Arid conditions favor salt accumulation. This is especially apparent when soil parent material is saline. Irrigation of arid lands is especially problematic. All irrigation water has some level of salinity. Irrigation, especially when it involves leakage from canals, often raise the underlying water table. Rapid salination occurs when the land surface is within the capillary fringe of saline groundwater. Soil salinity control involves flushing with higher levels of applied water in combination with tile drainage.

3 Mineral

A mineral is a naturally occurring solid formed through geological processes that has a characteristic chemical composition, a highly ordered atomic structure, and specific physical properties. A rock, by comparison, is an aggregate of minerals and/or mineraloids, and need not have a specific chemical composition. Minerals range in composition from pure elements and simple salts to very complex silicates with thousands of known forms. The study of minerals is called mineralogy.

Definition and Classification

To be classified as a true mineral, a substance must be a solid and have a crystalline structure. It must also be a naturally occurring, homogeneous substance with a defined chemical composition. Traditional definitions excluded organically derived material. However, the International Mineralogical Association in 1995 adopted a new definition:

- A mineral is an element or chemical compound that is normally crystalline and that has been formed as a result of geological processes.

The modern classifications include an organic class — in both the New Dana and the Strunz Classification schemes.

The chemical composition may vary between end members of a mineral system. For example the plagioclase feldspars comprise a continuous series from sodium and silicon-rich albite ($NaAlSi_3O_8$) to calcium and aluminium-rich anorthite ($CaAl_2Si_2O_8$) with four recognized intermediate compositions between. Mineral-like substances that don't strictly meet the definition are sometimes classified as mineraloids. Other natural-occurring substances are non-minerals. Industrial minerals is a market term and refers to commercially valuable mined materials.

A *crystal structure* is the orderly geometric spatial arrangement of atoms in the internal structure of a mineral. There are 14 basic crystal lattice arrangements of atoms in three dimensions, and these are referred to as the 14 Bravais lattices'. Each of these lattices can be classified into one of the seven crystal systems, and all crystal structures currently recognized fit in one Bravais lattice and one crystal system. This crystal structure is based on regular internal atomic or ionic arrangement that is often expressed in the geometric form that the crystal takes. Even when the mineral grains are too small to see or are irregularly shaped, the underlying crystal structure is always periodic and can be determined by X-ray diffraction. Chemistry and crystal structure together define a mineral. In fact, two or more minerals may have the same chemical composition, but differ in crystal structure (these are known as *polymorphs*). For example, pyrite and marcasite are both iron sulfide, but their arrangement of atoms differs. Similarly, some minerals have different chemical compositions, but the same crystal structure: for example, halite (made from sodium and chlorine), galena (made from lead and sulfur) and periclase (made from magnesium and oxygen) all share the same cubic crystal structure.

Crystal structure greatly influences a mineral's physical properties. For example, though diamond and graphite have the same composition (both are pure carbon), graphite is very soft, while diamond is the hardest of all known minerals. This happens because the carbon atoms in graphite are arranged into sheets which can slide easily past each other, while the carbon atoms in diamond form a strong, interlocking three-dimensional network.

There are currently more than 4,000 known minerals, according to the International Mineralogical Association, which is responsible for the approval of and naming of new mineral species found in nature. Of these, perhaps 100 can be called 'common', 50 are 'occasional', and the rest are 'rare' to 'extremely rare'. Without more recycling, zinc could be used up by 2037, both indium and hafnium could run out by 2017, and terbium could be gone before 2012.

Differences Between Minerals and Rocks

A mineral is a naturally occurring solid with a definite chemical composition and a specific crystalline structure. A rock is an aggregate of one or more minerals. (A rock may also include organic remains and mineraloids.) Some rocks are predominantly composed of just one mineral. For example, limestone is a sedimentary rock composed almost entirely of the mineral calcite. Other rocks contain many minerals, and the specific minerals in a rock can vary widely. Some minerals, like quartz, mica or feldspar are common, while others have been found in only four or five locations worldwide. The vast majority of the rocks of the Earth's crust consist of quartz, feldspar, mica, chlorite, kaolin, calcite, epidote, olivine, augite, hornblende, magnetite, hematite, limonite and a few other minerals. Over half of the mineral species known are so rare that they have only been found in a handful of samples, and many are known from only one or two small grains.

Commercially valuable minerals and rocks are referred to as industrial minerals. Rocks from which minerals are mined for economic purposes are referred to as ores (the rocks and minerals that remain, after the desired mineral has been separated from the ore, are referred to as tailings).

Mineral Composition of Rocks

A main determining factor in the formation of minerals in a rock mass is the chemical composition of the mass, for a certain mineral can be formed only when the necessary elements are present in the rock. Calcite is most common in limestones, as these consist essentially of calcium carbonate; quartz is common in sandstones and in certain igneous rocks which contain a high percentage of silica.

Other factors are of equal importance in determining the natural association or paragenesis of rock-forming minerals, principally the mode of origin of the rock and the stages through which it has passed in attaining its present condition. Two rock masses may have very much the same bulk composition and yet consist of entirely different assemblages of minerals. The tendency is always for those compounds to be formed which are stable under the conditions under which the rock mass originated. A granite arises by the consolidation of a molten magma at high temperatures and great pressures and its component minerals are those stable under such conditions.

Exposed to moisture, carbonic acid and other subaerial agents at the ordinary temperatures of the Earth's surface, some of these original minerals, such as quartz and white mica are relatively stable and remain unaffected; others weather or decay and are replaced by new combinations. The feldspar passes into kaolinite, muscovite and quartz, and any mafic minerals such as pyroxenes, amphiboles or biotite have been present they are often altered to chlorite, epidote, rutile and other substances. These changes are accompanied by disintegration, and the rock falls into a loose, incoherent, earthy mass which may be regarded as a sand or soil. The materials thus formed may be washed away and deposited as sandstone or siltstone. The structure of the original rock is now replaced by a new one; the mineralogical constitution is profoundly altered; but the bulk chemical composition may not be very different. The sedimentary rock may again undergo metamorphism. If penetrated by igneous rocks it may be recrystallized or, if subjected to enormous pressures with heat and movement during mountain building, it may be converted into a gneiss not very different in mineralogical composition though radically different in structure to the granite which was its original state.

Physical Properties of Minerals

Classifying minerals can range from simple to very difficult. A mineral can be identified by several physical properties, some of them being sufficient for full identification without equivocation. In other cases, minerals can only be classified by more complex chemical or X-ray diffraction analysis; these methods, however, can be costly and time-consuming.

Physical properties commonly used are:

- *Crystal structure and habit*: See the above discussion of crystal structure. A mineral may show good crystal habit or form, or it may be massive, granular or compact with only microscopically visible crystals.
- *Hardness*: the physical hardness of a mineral is usually measured according to the Mohs scale. This scale is relative and goes from 1 to 10. Minerals with a given Mohs hardness can scratch the surface of any mineral that has a lower hardness than itself.

  Mohs hardness scale:

- Talc $Mg_3Si_4O_{10}(OH)_2$
- Gypsum $CaSO_4{\cdot}2H_2O$
- Calcite $CaCO_3$
- Fluorite CaF_2
- Apatite $Ca_5(PO_4)_3$ (OH, Cl,F)
- Orthoclase $KAlSi_3O_8$
- Quartz SiO_2

- Topaz $Al_2SiO_4(OH,F)_2$
- Corundum Al_2O_3
- Diamond C (Pure carbon)

Luster indicates the way a mineral's surface interacts with light and can range from dull to glassy (vitreous).

Metallic — high reflectivity like metal: galena and pyrite

Sub-metallic — slightly less than metallic reflectivity: magnetite.

Non-metallic Lusters

- *Adamantine* — brilliant, the luster of diamond also cerussite and anglesite
- *Vitreous* — the luster of a broken glass quartz.
- *Pearly* — iridescent and pearl-like: talc and apophyllite.
- *Resinous* — the luster of resin: sphalerite and sulfur.
- *Silky* — a soft light shown by fibrous materials: gypsum and chrysotile.
- *Dull/earthy* — shown by finely crystallized minerals: the kidney ore variety of hematite.
- *Colour* indicates the appearance of the mineral in reflected light or transmitted light for translucent minerals (i.e. what it looks like to the naked eye).
- *Iridescence* — the play of colours due to surface or internal interference. Labradorite exhibits internal iridescence whereas hematite and sphalerite often show the surface effect.
- *Streak* refers to the colour of the powder a mineral leaves after rubbing it on an unglazed porcelain streak plate. Note that this is not always the same colour as the original mineral.
- *Cleavage* describes the way a mineral may split apart along various planes. In thin sections, cleavage is visible as thin parallel lines across a mineral.

- *Fracture* describes how a mineral breaks when broken contrary to its natural cleavage planes.
- *Chonchoidal fracture* is a smooth curved fracture with concentric ridges of the type shown by glass.
- *Hackley* is jagged fracture with sharp edges.
- *Fibrous*
- *Irregular*
- *Specific gravity* relates the mineral mass to the mass of an equal volume of water, namely the density of the material. While most minerals, including all the common rock-forming minerals, have a specific gravity of 2.5-3.5, a few are noticeably more or less dense, e.g. several sulfide minerals have high specific gravity compared to the common rock-forming minerals.

Other Properties

Fluorescence (response to ultraviolet light), magnetism, radioactivity, tenacity (response to mechanical induced changes of shape or form), piezoelectricity and reactivity to dilute acids.

Chemical Properties of Minerals

Minerals may be classified according to chemical composition. They are here categorized by anion group. The list below is in approximate order of their abundance in the Earth's crust. The list follows the Dana classification system which closely parallels the Strunz classification.

Silicate Class

The largest group of minerals by far are the silicates (most rocks are 95% silicates), which are composed largely of silicon and oxygen, with the addition of ions such as aluminium, magnesium, iron, and calcium. Some important rock-forming silicates include the feldspars, quartz, olivines, pyroxenes, amphiboles, garnets, and micas.

Carbonate Class

The carbonate minerals consist of those minerals containing the anion $(CO_3)^{2-}$ and include calcite and aragonite (both calcium carbonate), dolomite (magnesium/calcium carbonate) and siderite (iron carbonate). Carbonates are commonly deposited in marine settings when the shells of dead planktonic life settle and accumulate on the sea floor. Carbonates are also found in evaporitic settings (e.g. the Great Salt Lake, Utah) and also in karst regions, where the dissolution and reprecipitation of carbonates leads to the formation of caves, stalactites and stalagmites. The carbonate class also includes the nitrate and borate minerals.

Sulfate Class

Sulfate minerals all contain the sulfate anion, SO_4^{2-}. Sulfates commonly form in evaporitic settings where highly saline waters slowly evaporate, allowing the formation of both sulfates and halides at the water-sediment interface. Sulfates also occur in hydrothermal vein systems as gangue minerals along with sulfide ore minerals. Another occurrence is as secondary oxidation products of original sulfide minerals. Common sulfates include anhydrite (calcium sulfate), celestine (strontium sulfate), barite (barium sulfate), and gypsum (hydrated calcium sulfate). The sulfate class also includes the chromate, molybdate, selenate, sulfite, tellurate, and tungstate minerals.

Sulfide Class

Many sulfide minerals are economically important as metal ores. Common sulfides include pyrite (iron sulfide — commonly known as *fools' gold*), chalcopyrite (copper iron sulfide), pentlandite (nickel iron sulfide), and galena (lead sulfide). The sulfide class also includes the selenides, the tellurides, the arsenides, the antimonides, the bismuthinides, and the sulfosalts (sulfur and a second anion such as arsenic).

Phosphate Class

The phosphate mineral group actually includes any mineral with a tetrahedral unit AO_4 where A can be phosphorus, antimony, arsenic or vanadium. By far the most common phosphate is apatite which is an important biological mineral found in teeth and bones of many animals. The phosphate class includes the phosphate, arsenate, vanadate, and antimonate minerals.

Element Class

The elemental group includes metals and intermetallic elements (gold, silver, copper), semi-metals and non-metals (antimony, bismuth, graphite, sulfur). This group also includes natural alloys, such as electrum (a natural alloy of gold and silver), phosphides, silicides, nitrides and carbides (which are usually only found naturally in a few rare meteorites).

Organic Class

The organic mineral class includes biogenic substances in which geological processes have been a part of the genesis or origin of the existing compound. Minerals of the organic class include various oxalates, mellitates, citrates, cyanates, acetates, formates, hydrocarbons and other miscellaneous species. Examples include whewellite, moolooite, mellite, fichtelite, carpathite, evenkite and abelsonite.

Halide Class

The halide minerals are the group of minerals forming the natural salts and include fluorite (calcium fluoride), halite (sodium chloride), sylvite (potassium chloride), and sal ammoniac (ammonium chloride). Halides, like sulfates, are commonly found in evaporite settings such as salt lakes and landlocked seas such as the Dead Sea and Great Salt Lake. The halide class includes the fluoride, chloride, bromide and iodide minerals.

Oxide Class

Oxide minerals are extremely important in mining as they form many of the ores from which valuable metals can be extracted. They also carry the best record of changes in the Earth's magnetic field. They commonly occur as precipitates close to the Earth's surface, oxidation products of other minerals in the near surface weathering zone, and as accessory minerals in igneous rocks of the crust and mantle. Common oxides include hematite (iron oxide), magnetite (iron oxide), chromite (iron chromium oxide), spinel (magnesium aluminium oxide – a common component of the mantle), ilmenite (iron titanium oxide), rutile (titanium dioxide), and ice (hydrogen oxide). The oxide class includes the oxide and the hydroxide minerals.

4 Ore

An ore is a type of rock that contains minerals with important elements including metals. The ores are extracted through mining; these are then refined to extract the valuable element(s).

The grade or concentration of an ore mineral, or metal, as well as its form of occurrence, will directly affect the costs associated with mining the ore. The cost of extraction must thus be weighted against the contained metal value of the rock to determine what ore can be profitably extracted and what ore is of too low a grade to be worth mining. Metal ores are generally oxides, sulfides, silicates, or 'native' metals (such as native copper) that are not commonly concentrated in the Earth's crust or 'noble' metals (not usually forming compounds) such as gold. The ores must be processed to extract the metals of interest from the waste rock and from the ore minerals. Ore bodies are formed by a variety of geological processes. The process of ore formation is called ore genesis.

Ore Deposits

An ore deposit is an accumulation of ore. This is distinct from a mineral resource as defined by the mineral resource classification criteria. An ore deposit is one occurrence of the particular ore type. Most ore deposits are named according to either their location (for example, the Witswatersrand, South Africa), or after a discoverer (e.g. the kambalda nickel shoots are named after drillers), or after some whimsy, an historical figure, a prominent person, something from mythology (phoenix, kraken, serepentleopard, etc) or the code name of the resource company which found it (e.g. MKD-5 is the in-house name for the Mount Keith nickel).

Classification of Ore Deposits

Ore deposits are classified according to various criteria developed via the study of economic geology, or ore genesis. The classifications below are typical.

Hydrothermal Epigenetic Deposits

Mesothermal lode gold deposits, typified by the Golden Mile, Kalgoorlie.

Archaean conglomerate hosted gold-uranium deposits, typified by Elliot Lake, Canada and Witwatersrand, South Africa.

Carlin type gold deposits, including:

- Dolomite-hosted jasperoid replacement subtype
- *Epithermal* stockwork vein deposits

Granite Related Hydrothermal

IOCG or iron oxide copper gold deposits, typified by the supergiant Olympic Dam Cu-Au-U deposit

Porphyry copper +/- gold +/- molybdenum +/- silver deposits

Intrusive-related copper-gold +/- (tin-tungsten), typified by the Tombstone, Arizona deposits

Hydromagmatic magnetite iron ore deposits and skarns

Skarn ore deposits of copper, lead, zinc, tungsten, etcetera

Nickel-cobalt-platinum Deposits

Magmatic nickel-copper-iron-PGE deposits including:

- Cumulate vanadiferous or platinum-bearing magnetite or chromite
- Cumulate hard-rock titanium (ilmenite) deposits
- Komatiite hosted Ni-Cu-PGE deposits
- Subvolcanic feeder subtype, typified by Noril'sk-Talnakh and the Thompson Belt, Canada
- Intrusive-related Ni-Cu-PGE, typified by Voisey's Bay, Canada and Jinchuan, China
- Lateritic nickel ore deposits, examples include Goro and Acoje, (Philippines) and Ravensthorpe, Western Australia.

Volcanic-related Deposits

Volcanic hosted massive sulfide (VHMS) Cu-Pb-Zn including:

- Examples include Teutonic Bore and Golden Grove, Western Australia
- Besshi type
- Kuroko type

Metamorphically Reworked Deposits

Podiform serpentinite-hosted paramagmatic ron oxide-chromite deposits, typified by Savage River, Tasmania iron ore, Coobina chromite deposit.

Broken Hill Type Pb-Zn-Ag, considered to be a class of reworked SEDEX deposits.

Carbonatite-alkaline Igneous Related

- Phosphorus - tantalite - vermiculite (Phalaborwa South Africa)
- Rare earth elements — Mount Weld Australia and Bayan Obo, Mongolia

- Diatreme hosted diamond in kimberlite, lamproite or lamprophyre

Sedimentary Deposits

Close-up of Banded Iron Formation specimen from Upper Michigan. Scale bar is 5.0 mm.

Banded iron formation iron ore deposits, including:

- Channel-iron deposits or pisolite type iron ore
- Heavy mineral sands ore deposits and other sand dune hosted deposits
- Alluvial gold, diamond, tin, platinum or black sand deposits
- Alluvial oxide zinc deposit type: sole example Skorpion Zinc

SEDIMENTARY HYDROTHERMAL DEPOSITS

Sedex

- Lead-zinc-silver, typified by Red Dog, McArthur River, Mount Isa, etc.
- Stratiform arkose-hosted and shale-hosted copper, typified by the Zambian copperbelt.
- Stratiform tungsten, typified by the Erzgebirge deposits, Czechoslovakia.
- Exhalative spilite-chert hosted gold deposits.
- Mississippi valley type (MVT) zinc-lead deposits.
- Hematite iron ore deposits of altered banded iron formation.

Extraction

The basic extraction of ore deposits follows the steps below:

- Prospecting or Exploration to find and then define the extent and value of ore where it is located ('ore body')

- Conduct resource estimation to mathematically estimate the size and grade of the deposit.
- Conduct a pre-feasibility study to determine the theoretical economics of the ore deposit. This identifies, early on, whether further investment in estimation and engineering studies is warranted and identifies key risks and areas for further work.
- Conduct a feasibility study to evaluate the financial viability, technical and financial risks and robustness of the project and make a decision as whether to develop or walk away from a proposed mine project. This includes mine planning to evaluate the economically recoverable portion of the deposit, the metallurgy and ore recoverability, marketability and payability of the ore concentrates, engineering, milling and infrastructure costs, finance and equity requirements and a cradle to grave analysis of the possible mine, from the initial excavation all the way through to reclamation.

Development to create access to an ore body and building of mine plant and equipment.

The operation of the mine in an active sense.

Reclamation to make land where a mine had been suitable for future use.

Ores (metals) are traded internationally and comprise a sizeable portion of international trade in raw materials both in value and volume. This is because the worldwide distribution of ores is unequal and dislocated from locations of peak demand and from smelting infrastructure.

Most base metals (copper, lead, zinc, nickel) are traded internationally on the London Metal Exchange, with smaller stockpiles and metals exchanges monitored by the COMEX and NYMEX exchanges in the United States and the Shanghai Futures Exchange in China.

Iron ore is traded between customer and producer, though various benchmark prices are set yearly between the major mining conglomerates and the major consumers, and this sets the stage for smaller participants.

Other, lesser, commodities do not have international clearing houses and benchmark prices, with most prices negotiated between suppliers and customers one-on-one. This generally makes determining the price of ores of this nature opaque and difficult. Such metals include lithium, niobium-tantalum, bismuth, antimony and rare earths. Most of these commodities are also dominated by one or two major suppliers with >60 per cent of the world's reserves. The London Metal Exchange aims to add uranium to its list of metals on warrant.

The World Bank reports that China was the top importer of ores and metals in 2005 followed by the USA and Japan.

Important Ore Minerals

- *Acanthite:* Ag_2S for production of silver
- *Barite*: $BaSO_4$
- Bauxite Al_2O_3 for production of aluminium
- Beryl: $Be_3Al_2(SiO_3)_6$
- Bornite: Cu_5FeS_4
- Cassiterite: SnO_2
- Chalcocite: Cu_2S for production of copper
- Chalcopyrite: $CuFeS_2$
- Chromite: $(Fe, Mg)Cr_2O_4$ for production of chromium
- Cinnabar: HgS for production of mercury
- Cobaltite: (Co, Fe)AsS
- Columbite-Tantalite or Coltan: $(Fe, Mn)(Nb, Ta)_2O_6$
- Galena: PbS

- Gold: Au, typically associated with quartz or as placer deposits
- Hematite: Fe_2O_3
- Ilmenite: $FeTiO_3$
- Magnetite: Fe_3O_4
- Molybdenite: MoS_2
- Pentlandite:$(Fe, Ni)_9S_8$
- Pyrolusite:MnO_2
- Scheelite: $CaWO_4$
- Sphalerite: ZnS
- Uraninite (pitchblende): UO_2 for production of metallic uranium
- Wolframite: $(Fe, Mn) WO_4$

5 Soil Fertility

Soil is the characteristics that supports life. The term, soil, is used to describe agriculture and garden life.

Fertile soil has the following properties:

- It is rich in nutrients necessary for basic plant nutrition, including nitrogen, phosphorus and potassium.
- It contains sufficient minerals (trace elements) for plant nutrition, including boron, chlorine, cobalt, copper, iron, manganese, magnesium, molybdenum, sulfur, and zinc.
- It contains soil organic matter that improves soil structure and soil moisture retention.
- Soil pH is in the range 6.0 to 6.8.
- Good soil structure, creating well drained soil.
- A range of microorganisms that support plant growth.
- It often contains large amounts of topsoil.

In lands used for agriculture and other human activities, fertile soil typically arises from the use of soil conservation practices.

Soil Fertilization

Nitrogen is the element in the soil that is most often lacking. Phosphorus and potassium are also needed in substantial amounts. For this reason these three elements are always included in commercial fertilizers and the content of each of these items is included on the bags of fertilizer. For example a 10-10-15 fertilizer has 10 per cent nitrogen, 10 per cent (P_2O_5) available phosphorus and 15 per cent (K_2O) water soluble potassium. Inorganic fertilizers are generally less expensive and have higher concentrations of nutrients than organic fertilizers. Some have criticized the use of inorganic fertilizers claiming that the water-soluble nitrogen doesn't provide for the long-term needs of the plant and creates water pollution. Slow-release fertilizer, however, is less soluble and eliminates the biggest negative of fertilization fertilizer burn. Additionally, most soluble fertilizers are coated, such as sulfur-coated urea.

In 2008, the cost of phosphorus as fertilizer more than doubled while the price of rock phosphate as base commodity rose 8-fold, recently the term peak phosphorus has been coined, due to the limited occurrence of rock phosphate in the world.

Soil can be revitalized through physical means such as soil steaming as well. Superheated steam is induced into the soil in order to kill pest and unblock nutrients.

Light and CO_2 Limitations

Photosynthesis is the process whereby plants use light energy to drive chemical reactions which convert CO_2 into sugars. As such, all plants require access to both light and carbon dioxide to produce energy, grow and reproduce.

While typically limited by nitrogen, phosphorus and potassium, low levels of carbon dioxide can also act as a limiting factor on plant growth. Peer reviewed and published scientific studies have shown that increasing CO_2 is highly effective at promoting plant growth up to levels over 300ppm. Further increases in CO_2 can, to a very small degree, continue to increase net photosynthetic output.

Since higher levels of CO_2 have only a minimal impact on photosynthetic output at present levels (presently around 380 ppm and increasing), we should not consider plant growth to be limited by carbon dioxide. Other biochemical limitations, such as soil organic content, nitrogen in the soil, phosphorus and potassium, are far more often in short supply. As such, neither commercial nor scientific communities look to air fertilization as an effective or economic method of increasing production in agriculture or natural ecosystems. Furthermore, since microbial decomposition occurs faster under warmer temperatures, higher levels of CO_2 (which is one of the causes of unusually fast climate change) should be expected to increase the rate at which nutrients are leached out of soils and may have a negative impact on soil fertility.

Soil Depletion

Soil depletion occurs when the components which contribute to fertility are removed and not replaced, and the conditions which support soil fertility are not maintained. This leads to poor crop yields. In agriculture, depletion can be due to excessively intense cultivation and inadequate soil management.

One of the most widespread occurrences of soil depletion as of 2008 is in tropical zones where nutrient content of soils is low. The combined effects of growing population densities, large-scale industrial logging, slash-and-burn agriculture and ranching, and other factors, have in some places depleted soils through rapid and almost total nutrient removal.

Topsoil depletion is when the nutrient rich organic topsoil that takes hundreds to thousands of years to build up under natural conditions is eroded or depleted of its original organic material. Historically, many past civilizations collapses can be attributed to the depletion of the topsoil. Since the beginning of agricultural production in the Great

Plains of North America in the 1880s about one half of its topsoil has disappeared.

Depletion may occur through a variety of other effects, including overtillage which damages soil structure, overuse of inputs such as synthetic fertilizers and herbicides, which leave residues and buildups that inhibit microorganisms, and salinization of soil.

Humus

Humus (origin: 1790-1800; < *Latin*: earth, ground) is degraded organic material in soil, which causes some soil layers to be dark brown or black.

In soil science, humus refers to any organic matter that has reached a point of stability, where it will break down no further and might, if conditions do not change, remain essentially as it is for centuries, if not millennia.

In agriculture, humus is sometimes also used to describe mature compost, or natural compost extracted from a forest or other spontaneous source for use to amend soil. It is also used to describe a topsoil horizon that contains organic matter (humus type, humus form).

HUMIFICATION

Transformation of Organic Matter into Humus

The process of 'humification' can occur naturally in soil, or in the production of compost. The importance of chemically stable humus is thought by some to be the fertility it provides to soils in both a physical and chemical sense, though some agricultural experts put a greater focus on other features of it, such as disease suppressiveness. Physically, it helps the soil retain moisture by increasing microporosity, and encourages the formation of good soil structure. Chemically, the incorporation of oxygen into large organic molecular assemblages generates many active, negatively charged sites that bind to positively charged ions (cations) of plant nutrients, making them more available by ion exchange. Biologically, it allows soil organisms (microbes and animals) to feed and reproduce. Humus is often described as the 'life-force' of the soil. Yet, it is difficult to define humus in precise terms; it is a highly complex substance, the full nature of which is still not fully understood. Physically, humus can be differentiated from organic matter in that the latter is rough looking material, with coarse plant remains still visible, while once fully humified organic matter becomes more uniform in appearance (a dark, spongy, jelly-like substance) and amorphous in structure, and may remain such for millennia or more. That is, it has no determinate shape, structure or character. However, humified organic matter, when examined under the microscope without any chemical treatment, may reveal tiny but clearly identifiable plant, animal or microbial remains which have been mechanically, but not chemically degraded . This points to a fuzzy limit between humus and organic matter. In most recent literature, humus is clearly considered as an integral part of soil organic matter (SOM).

Plant remains (including those that passed through an animal gut and were excreted as faeces) contain organic compounds: sugars, starches, proteins, carbohydrates, lignins, waxes, resins and organic acids. The process of organic matter decay in the soil begins with the decomposition of sugars and starches from carbohydrates, which break down easily as saprotrophs initially invade the dead plant organs, while the remaining cellulose and lignin break down more slowly. Simple proteins, organic acids, starches and sugars break down rapidly, while crude proteins, fats, waxes and resins remain relatively unchanged for longer periods of time. Lignin, which is slowly transformed by white-rot fungi, is one of the main precursors of humus, together with by-products of microbial nd animal activity. The humus, that is the end product of this manifold process, is thus a mixture of compounds and complex life chemicals of plant, animal, or microbial origin, which has many functions and benefits in the soil. Most humus in the soil is included in animal faeces of more or less dark colour according to their content in organic matter. Earthworm humus (vermicompost) is considered by some to be the best organic manure there is.

Stability of Humus

Compost that is readily capable of further decomposition is sometimes referred to as effective or active humus, though again scientists would say that if it is not stable, it's not humus at all. This kind of compost, rich in plant remains and fulvic acids, is an excellent source of plant nutrients, but of little value regarding long-term soil structure and tilth. Stable (or passive) humus consisting of humic acids and humins, on the other hand, are so highly insoluble (or so tightly bound to clay particles and hydroxides) that they cannot be penetrated by microbes and therefore are greatly resistant to further decomposition. Thus stable humus adds few readily available nutrients to the soil, but plays an essential part in providing its physical structure. Some very stable humus complexes have survived for thousands of years. The most stable humus is that formed from the slow oxidation of black carbon, after the incorporation of finely powdered charcoal into the topsoil. This process is at the origin of the formation of the fertile Amazonian Dark Earths or Terra preta de Indio.

Humus is transformed by soil organisms, which may contribute to increase or decrease its stability according to their enzyme equipment. The disappearance of humus is hastened by warm and moist climate, which explains why most tropical soils are so poor in organic matter and suffer from both lack of good structure and available nutrients. In boreal countries and at high altitudes, the lack of active transformation of organic matter into humus, because of harsh climate conditions, leads to a similar decrease in soil fertility, although for opposite reasons. Among other factors, this explains why temperate climates were most favourable to the development of sedentary agriculture in the past millennia, before the advent of mineral fertilizers.

Benefits of Soil Organic Matter and Humus

- The mineralization process that converts raw organic matter to the relatively stable substance that is humus feeds the soil population of micro-organisms and other creatures, thus maintaining high and healthy levels of soil life.
- The rate at which raw organic matter is converted into humus promotes (when fast) or limits (when slow) the coexistence of plants, animals and microbes in terrestrial ecosystems.
- Effective and stable humus (*see below*) are further sources of nutrients to microbes, the former providing a readily available supply while the latter acts as a more long-term storage reservoir.

Decomposition of dead plant material causes complex organic compounds to be slowly oxidized (lignin-like humus) or to break down into simpler forms (sugars and amino-sugars, aliphatic and phenolic organic acids) which are further transformed into microbial biomass (microbial humus) or are reorganized (and still oxidized) in humic assemblages (fulvic and humic acids, humins) which bind to clay minerals and metal hydroxides. There has been a long debate about the ability of plants to uptake humic substances from their root systems and to metabolize them. There is now a consensus about humus as playing a hormonal role rather than a nutritional role in plant physiology. Humus is a colloidal substance, and increases the soil's cation exchange capacity, hence its ability to store nutrients by chelation as can clay particles; thus while these nutrient cations are accessible to plants, they are held in the soil safe from leaching away by rain or irrigation. Humus can hold the equivalent of 80-90 per cent of its weight in moisture, and therefore increases the soil's capacity to withstand drought conditions. The biochemical structure of humus enables it to moderate — or buffer — excessive acid or alkaline soil conditions. During the humification process, microbes (bacteria and fungi) secrete sticky gums and mucilages; these contribute to the crumb structure of the soil by holding particles together, allowing greater aeration of the soil. Toxic substances such as heavy metals, as well as excess nutrients, can be chelated (that is, bound to the complex organic molecules of humus) and prevented from entering the wider ecosystem, thereby detoxifying it. The dark colour of humus (usually black or dark brown) helps to warm up cold soils in the spring.

Biomass

Biomass, a renewable energy source, is biological material derived from living, or recently living organisms, such as wood, waste, and alcohol fuels. Biomass is commonly plant matter grown to generate electricity or produce heat. For example, forest residues (such as dead trees, branches and tree stumps), yard clippings and wood chips and garbage may be used as biomass. However, biomass also includes plant or animal matter used for production of fibers or chemicals. Biomass may also include biodegradable wastes that can be burnt as fuel. It excludes organic materials such as fossil fuels which have been transformed by geological processes into substances such as coal or petroleum.

Industrial biomass can be grown from numerous types of plants, including miscanthus, switchgrass, hemp, corn, poplar, willow, sorghum, sugarcane, and a variety of tree species, ranging from eucalyptus to oil palm (palm oil). The particular plant used is usually not important to the end products, but it does affect the processing of the raw material.

Although fossil fuels have their origin in ancient biomass, they are not considered biomass by the generally accepted definition because they contain carbon that has been 'out' of the carbon cycle for a very long time. Their combustion therefore disturbs the carbon dioxide content in the atmosphere.

Plastics from biomass, like some recently developed to dissolve in seawater, are made the same way as petroleum-based plastics. These plastics are actually cheaper to manufacture and meet or exceed most performance standards, but they lack the same water resistance or longevity as conventional plastics.

Chemical Composition

Biomass is carbon based and is composed of a mixture of organic molecules containing hydrogen, usually including atoms of oxygen, often nitrogen and also small quantities of other atoms, including alkali, alkaline earth and heavy metals. These metals are often found in functional molecules such as the porphyrins which include chlorophyll which contains magnesium.

Biomass Sources

Biomass energy is derived from five distinct energy sources: garbage, wood, waste, landfill gases, and alcohol fuels. Wood energy is derived both from direct use of harvested wood as a fuel and from wood waste streams. The largest source of energy from wood is pulping liquor or 'black liquor', a waste product from processes of the pulp, paper and paperboard industry. Waste energy is the second-largest source of biomass energy. The main contributors of waste energy are municipal solid waste (MSW), manufacturing waste, and landfill gas. Biomass alcohol fuel, or ethanol, is derived almost exclusively from corn. Its principal use is as an oxygenate in gasoline.

Biomass can be converted to other usable forms of energy like methane gas or transportation fuels like ethanol and biodiesel. Methane gas is the main ingredient of natural gas. Smelly stuff, like rotting garbage, and agricultural and human waste, release methane gas — also called 'landfill gas' or 'biogas'. Crops like corn and sugar cane can be fermented to produce the transportation fuel, ethanol. Biodiesel, another transportation fuel, can be produced from left-over food products like vegetable oils and animal fats. Also, Biomass to liquids (BTLs) and cellulosic ethanol are still under research.

Biomass Conversion Process to Useful Energy

There are a number of technological options available to make use of a wide variety of biomass types as a renewable energy source. Conversion technologies may release the energy directly, in the form of heat or electricity, or may convert it to another form, such as liquid biofuel or combustible biogas. While for some classes of biomass resource there may be a number of usage options, for others there may be only one appropriate technology.

Thermal Conversion

These are processes in which heat is the dominant mechanism to convert the biomass into another chemical form. The basic alternatives are separated principally by the extent to which the chemical reactions involved are allowed to proceed: Combustion, Torrefaction, Pyrolysis, Gasification.

There are a number of other less common, more experimental or proprietary thermal processes that may offer benefits such as hydrothermal upgrading (HTU) and hydroprocessing. Some have been developed for use on high moisture content biomass, including aqueous slurries, and allow them to be converted into more convenient forms. Some of the Applications of thermal conversion are Combined heat and power (CHP) and Co-firing. In a typical biomass power plant, efficiencies range from 20-27 per cent.

Chemical Conversion

A range of chemical processes may be used to convert biomass into other forms, such as to produce a fuel that is more conveniently used, transported or stored, or to exploit some property of the process itself.

Biochemical Conversion

As biomass is a natural material, many highly efficient biochemical processes have developed in nature to break down the molecules of which biomass is composed, and many of these biochemical conversion processes can be harnessed.

Biochemical conversion makes use of the enzymes of bacteria and other micro-organisms to break down biomass. In most cases micro-organisms are used to perform the conversion process: anaerobic digestion, fermentation and composting. Other chemical processes such as converting straight and waste vegetable oils into biodiesel is transesterification. Another way of breaking down biomass is by breaking down the carbohydrates and simple sugars to make alcohol. However, this process has not been perfected yet. Scientists are still researching the effects of converting biomass.

Environmental Impact

On combustion the carbon from biomass is released into the atmosphere as carbon dioxide (CO_2). The amount of carbon stored in dry wood is approximately 50 per cent by weight. When from agricultural sources, plant matter used as a fuel can be replaced by planting for new growth. When the biomass is from forests, the time to recapture the carbon stored is generally longer, and the carbon storage capacity of the forest may be reduced overall if destructive forestry techniques are employed.

The existing biomass power generating industry in the United States, which consists of approximately 11,000 MW (megawatts) of summer operating capacity actively supplying power to the grid, produces about 0.01 per cent of the U.S. electricity supply.

Currently, the New Hope Power Partnership is the largest biomass power plant in North America. The 140 MW facility uses sugar cane fiber (bagasse) and recycled urban wood as fuel to generate enough power for its large milling and refining operations as well as to supply renewable electricity for nearly 60,000 homes. The facility reduces dependence on oil by more than one million barrels per year, and by recycling sugar cane and wood waste, preserves landfill space in urban communities in Florida.

The amount of biomass available is usually not as great as stated in the example above. Many times, especially in Europe where large agricultural developments are not usual, the cost for transporting the biomass overcomes its actual value and therefore the gathering ground has to be limited to a certain small area. This fact leads to only small possible power outputs around 1 MW_{el}. To make an economic operation possible those power plants have to be equipped with the ORC technology, a cycle similar to the water steam power process just with an organic working medium. Such small power plants can be found in Europe.

Despite harvesting, biomass crops may sequester (trap) carbon. So for example soil organic carbon has been observed to be greater in switchgrass stands than in cultivated cropland soil, especially at depths below 12 inches. The grass sequesters the carbon in its increased root biomass. Typically, perennial crops sequester much more carbon than annual crops due to much greater non-harvested living biomass, both living and dead, built up over years, and much less soil disruption in cultivation.

The biomass-is-carbon-neutral proposal put forward in the early 1990's has been superseded by more recent science that recognizes that mature, intact forests sequester carbon more effectively than cut-over areas. When a tree's carbon is released into the atmosphere in a single pulse, it contributes to climate change much more than woodland timber rotting slowly over decades. Current studies indicate that recapturing carbon released by burning will take minimally hundreds of years.

Using biomass as a fuel produces the same air-pollution challenges as other fuels. Black carbon — a pollutant created by incomplete combustion of fossil fuels, biofuels, and biomass — is possibly the second largest contributor to global warming. In 2009 a Swedish study of the giant brown haze that periodically covers large areas in South Asia determined that it had been principally produced by biomass burning, and to a lesser extent by fossil-fuel burning. Researchers measured a significant concentration of ^{14}C, which is associated with recent plant life rather than with fossil fuels.

6 Fossil Fuel

Fossil fuels or gas fuels are fuels formed by natural resources such as anaerobic decomposition of buried dead organisms. The age of the organisms and their resulting fossil fuels is typically millions of years, and sometimes exceeds 650 million years. These fuels contain a high percentage of carbon and hydrocarbons.

Fossil fuels range from volatile materials with low carbon: hydrogen ratios like methane, to liquid petroleum to non-volatile materials composed of almost pure carbon, like anthracite coal. Methane can be found in hydrocarbon fields, alone, associated with oil, or in the form of methane clathrates. It is generally accepted that they formed from the fossilized remains of dead plants and animals by exposure to heat and pressure in the Earth's crust over hundreds of millions of years. This biogenic theory was first introduced by Georg Agricola in 1556 and later by Mikhail Lomonosov in the 18th century.

It was estimated by the Energy Information Administration that in 2007 primary sources of energy consisted of petroleum 36.0 per cent, coal 27.4 per cent, natural gas 23.0 per cent, amounting to an 86.4 per cent share for fossil fuels in primary energy consumption in the world.

Non-fossil sources in 2006 included hydroelectric 6.3 per cent, nuclear 8.5 per cent, and (geothermal, solar, tide, wind, wood, waste) amounting 0.9 per cent. World energy consumption was growing about 2.3 per cent per year.

Fossil fuels are non-renewable resources because they take millions of years to form, and reserves are being depleted much faster than new ones are being formed. The production and use of fossil fuels raise environmental concerns. A global movement toward the generation of renewable energy is therefore under way to help meet increased energy needs.

The burning of fossil fuels produces around 21.3 billion tonnes (21.3 gigatonnes) of carbon dioxide per year, but it is estimated that natural processes can only absorb about half of that amount, so there is a net increase of 10.65 billion tonnes of atmospheric carbon dioxide per year (one tonne of atmospheric carbon is equivalent to 44/12 or 3.7 tonnes of carbon dioxide). Carbon dioxide is one of the greenhouse gases that enhances radiative forcing and contributes to global warming, causing the average surface temperature of the Earth to rise in response, which climate scientists agree will cause major adverse effects.

Origin

Fossil fuels are formed by the anaerobic decomposition of remains of organisms including phytoplankton and zooplankton that settled to the sea (or lake) bottom in large quantities under anoxic conditions, millions of years ago. Over geological time, this organic matter, mixed with mud, got buried under heavy layers of sediment. The resulting high levels of heat and pressure caused the organic matter to chemically alter, first into a waxy material known as kerogen which is found in oil shales, and then with more heat into liquid and gaseous hydrocarbons in a process known as catagenesis.

There is a wide range of organic, or hydrocarbon, compounds in any given fuel mixture. The specific mixture of hydrocarbons gives a fuel its characteristic properties, such as boiling point, melting point, density, viscosity, etc. Some fuels like natural gas, for instance, contain only very low boiling, gaseous components. Others such as gasoline or diesel contain much higher boiling components.

Terrestrial plants, on the other hand, tend to form coal. Many of the coal fields date to the Carboniferous period of Earth's history. Terrestrial plants also form type III kerogen, a source of natural gas.

Fossil fuels are of great importance because they can be burned (oxidized to carbon dioxide and water), producing significant amounts of energy. The use of coal as a fuel predates recorded history. Coal was used to run furnaces for the melting of metal ore. Semi-solid hydrocarbons from seeps were also burned in ancient times but these materials were mostly used for waterproofing and embalming.

Commercial exploitation of petroleum, largely as a replacement for oils from animal sources (notably whale oil) for use in oil lamps began in the nineteenth century.

Natural gas, once flared-off as an un-needed byproduct of petroleum production, is now considered a very valuable resource.

Heavy crude oil, which is much more viscous than conventional crude oil, and tar sands, where bitumen is found mixed with sand and clay, are becoming more important as sources of fossil fuel. Oil shale and similar materials are sedimentary rocks containing kerogen, a complex mixture of high-molecular weight organic compounds, which yield synthetic crude oil when heated (pyrolyzed). These materials have yet to be exploited commercially. These fuels are employed in internal combustion engines, fossil fuel power stations and other uses.

Prior to the latter half of the eighteenth century, windmills or watermills provided the energy needed for industry such as milling flour, sawing wood or pumping water, and burning wood or peat provided domestic heat. The wide-scale use of fossil fuels, coal at first and petroleum later, to fire steam engines, enabled the Industrial Revolution. At the same time, gas lights using natural gas or coal gas were coming into wide use. The invention of the internal combustion engine and its use in automobiles and trucks greatly increased the demand for gasoline and diesel oil, both made from fossil fuels. Other forms of transportation, railways and aircraft also required fossil fuels. The other major use for fossil fuels is in generating electricity and the petrochemical industry. Tar, a leftover of petroleum extraction, is used in construction of roads.

Limits and Alternatives

The principle of supply and demand suggests that as hydrocarbon supplies diminish, prices will rise. Therefore higher prices will lead to increased alternative, renewable energy supplies as previously uneconomic sources become sufficiently economical to exploit. Artificial gasolines and other renewable energy sources currently require more expensive production and processing technologies than conventional petroleum reserves, but may become economically viable in the near future. See Energy development. Different alternative sources of energy include nuclear, hydroelectric, solar, wind, and geothermal.

Levels and Flows

Levels of primary energy sources are the reserves in the ground. Flows are production. The most important part of primary energy sources are the carbon based fossil energy sources. Oil, coal, and gas stood for 79.6 per cent of primary energy production during 2002 (in million tonnes of oil equivalent (mtoe)) (34.9+23.5+21.2).

Levels (proved reserves) during 2005-2007

Levels (proved reserves) during 2005-2007

- **Oil:** 1,119-1,317 billion barrels (178-209 billion m^3)
- **Gas:** 6,183-6,381 trillion cubic feet (175-181 trillion m^3), 1,161 billion barrel oil equivalent (BBOE)
- **Coal:** 997,748 million short tons (905 billion tonnes), 4,416 BBOE

Flows (daily production) during 2006

- **Oil:** 84 million barrels per day (13 million m^3)
- **Gas:** 104,435 billion cubic feet (2,960 billion m^3), 19 million barrels oil equivalent per day (MBOED)
- **Coal:** 18,476,127 short tons (16,761,260 tonnes), 52 MBOED

Years of production left in the ground with the most optimistic proved reserve estimates (Oil & Gas Journal, World Oil).

- **Oil:** 43 years (43 years using levels and flows above)
- **Gas:** 167 years (61 years using levels and flows above)
- **Coal:** 417 years (148 years using levels and flows above)

Note that this calculation assumes that the product could be produced at a constant level for that number of years and that all of the proved reserves could be recovered. In reality, consumption of all three resources has been increasing. While this suggests that the resource will be used up more quickly, in reality, the production curve is much more akin to a bell curve. At some point in time, the production of each resource within an area, country, or globally will reach a maximum value, after which, the production will decline until it reaches a point where is no longer economically feasible or physically possible to produce. See Hubbert peak theory for detail on this decline curve with regard to petroleum. Note also that proved reserve estimates do not include strategic reserves, which (globally) amount to 4.1 billion more barrels.

The above discussion emphasizes worldwide energy balance. It is also valuable to understand the ratio of reserves to annual consumption (R/C) by region or country. For example, energy policy of the United Kingdom recognizes that Europe's R/C value is 3.0, very low by world standards, and exposes that region to energy vulnerability. Specific alternatives to fossil fuels are a subject of intense debate worldwide.

Environmental Effects

In the United States, more than 90 per cent of greenhouse gas emissions come from the combustion of fossil fuels. Combustion of fossil fuels also produces other air pollutants, such as nitrogen oxides, sulphur dioxide, volatile organic compounds and heavy metals.

According to Environment Canada:

> "The electricity sector is unique among industrial sectors in its very large contribution to emissions associated with nearly all air issues. Electricity generation produces a large share of Canadian nitrogen oxides and sulphur dioxide emissions, which contribute to smog and acid rain and the formation of fine particulate matter. It is the largest uncontrolled industrial source of mercury emissions in Canada. Fossil fuel-fired electric power plants also emit carbon dioxide, which may contribute to climate change. In addition, the sector has significant impacts on water and habitat and species. In particular, hydro dams and transmission lines have significant effects on water and biodiversity."

Carbon dioxide variations over the last 400,000 years, showing a rise since the industrial revolution.

According to U.S. Scientist Jerry Mahlman and USA Today:

> Mahlman, who crafted the IPCC language used to define levels of scientific certainty, says the new report will lay the blame at the feet of fossil fuels with 'virtual certainty', meaning 99 per cent sure. That's a significant jump from 'likely', or 66 per cent sure, in the group's last report in 2001, Mahlman says. His role in this year's effort involved spending two months reviewing the more than 1,600 pages of research that went into the new assessment.

Combustion of fossil fuels generates sulfuric, carbonic, and nitric acids, which fall to Earth as acid rain, impacting both natural areas and the built environment. Monuments and sculptures made from marble and limestone are particularly vulnerable, as the acids dissolve calcium carbonate.

Fossil fuels also contain radioactive materials, mainly uranium and thorium, which are released into the atmosphere. In 2000, about 12,000 tonnes of thorium and 5,000 tonnes of uranium were released worldwide from burning coal. It is estimated that during 1982, US coal burning released 155 times as much radioactivity into the atmosphere as the Three Mile Island incident. However, this radioactivity from coal burning is minuscule at each source and has not shown to have any adverse effect on human physiology.

Burning coal also generates large amounts of bottom ash and fly ash. These materials are used in a wide variety of applications, utilizing, for example, about 40 per cent of the US production.

Carbon Dioxide Variations Over the Last 400000 Years

Harvesting, processing, and distributing fossil fuels can also create environmental concerns. Coal mining methods, particularly mountaintop removal and strip mining, have

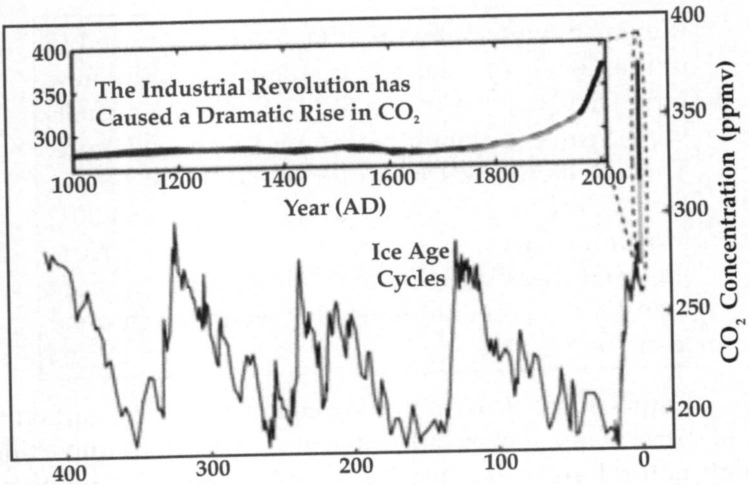

negative environmental impacts, and offshore oil drilling poses a hazard to aquatic organisms. Oil refineries also have negative environmental impacts, including air and water pollution. Transportation of coal requires the use of diesel-powered locomotives, while crude oil is typically transported by tanker ships, each of which requires the combustion of additional fossil fuels.

Environmental regulation uses a variety of approaches to limit these emissions, such as command-and-control (which mandates the amount of pollution or the technology used), economic incentives, or voluntary programmes.

An example of such regulation in the USA is the "EPA is implementing policies to reduce airborne mercury emissions. Under regulations issued in 2005, coal-fired power plants will need to reduce their emissions by 70 per cent by 2018."

In economic terms, pollution from fossil fuels is regarded as a negative externality. Taxation is considered one way to make societal costs explicit, in order to 'internalize' the cost of pollution. This aims to make fossil fuels more expensive, thereby reducing their use and the amount of pollution associated with them, along with raising the funds necessary to counteract these factors.

Former CIA Director James Woolsey recently outlined the national security arguments in favor of moving away from fossil fuels.

7 Pedology

Pedology (from Greek: *pedon*, 'soil'; and , *logos*, 'study') is the study of soils in their natural environment. It is one of two main branches of soil science, the other being edaphology. Pedology deals with pedogenesis, soil morphology, and soil classification, while edaphology studies the way soils influence plants, fungi, and other living things.

Soil is not only a support for vegetation, but it is also the zone (the pedosphere) of numerous interactions between climate (water, air, temperature), soil life (micro-organisms, plants, animals) and its residues, the mineral material of the original and added rock, and its position in the landscape. During its formation and genesis, the soil profile slowly deepens and develops characteristic layers, called 'horizons', while a steady state balance is approached.

Soil users (such as agronomists) showed initially little concern in the dynamics of soil. They saw it as medium whose chemical, physical and biological properties were useful for the services of agronomic productivity . On the other hand, pedologists and geologists did not initially focus on the agronomic applications of the soil characteristics (edaphic properties) but upon its relation to the nature and history of landscapes. Today, there's an integration of the two disciplinary approaches as part of landscape and environmental sciences.

Pedologists are now also interested in the practical applications of a good understanding of pedogenesis processes (the evolution and functioning of soils), like interpreting its environmental history and predicting consequences of changes in land use, while agronomists understand that the cultivated soil is a complex medium, often resulting from several thousands of years of evolution. They understand that the current balance is fragile and that only a thorough knowledge of its history makes it possible to ensure its sustainable use.

Concepts

Complexity in soil genesis is more common than simplicity.

Soils lie at the interface of Earth's atmosphere, biosphere, hydrosphere and lithosphere. Therefore, a thorough understanding of soils requires some knowledge of meteorology, climatology, ecology, biology, hydrology, geomorphology, geology and many other earth sciences and natural sciences.

Contemporary soils carry imprints of pedogenic processes that were active in the past, although in many cases these imprints are difficult to observe or quantify. Thus, knowledge of paleoecology, palaeogeography, glacial geology and paleoclimatology is important for the recognition and understanding of soil genesis and constitute a basis for predicting the future soil changes.

Five major, external factors of soil formation (climate, organisms, relief, parent material and time), and several smaller, less identifiable ones, drive pedogenic processes and create soil patterns.

Characteristics of soils and soil landscapes, e.g., the number, sizes, shapes and arrangements of soil bodies, each of which is characterized on the basis of soil horizons, degree of internal homogeneity, slope, aspect, landscape position, age and other properties and relationships, can be observed and measured. Distinctive bioclimatic regimes or combinations of pedogenic processes produce distinctive soils. Thus, distinctive, observable morphological features, e.g., illuvial clay accumulation in B horizons, are produced by certain combinations of pedogenic processes operative over varying periods of time. Pedogenic (soil-forming) processes act to both create and destroy order (anisotropy) within soils; these processes can proceed simultaneously. The resulting soil profile reflects the balance of these processes, present and past. The geological Principle of Uniformitarianism applies to soils, i.e., pedogenic processes active in soils today have been operating for long periods of time, back to the time of appearance of organisms on the land surface. These processes do, however, have varying degrees of expression and intensity over space and time. A succession of different soils may have developed, eroded and/or regressed at any particular site, as soil genetic factors and site factors, e.g., vegetation, sedimentation, geomorphology, change. There are very few old soils (in a geological sense) because they can be destroyed or buried by geological events, or modified by shifts in climate by virtue of their vulnerable position at the surface of the earth. Little of the soil continuum dates back beyond the Tertiary period and most soils and land surfaces are no older than the Pleistocene Epoch. However, preserved/lithified soils (paleosols) are an almost ubiqutious feature in terrestrial (land-based) environments throughout most of geologic time. Since they record evidence of ancient climate change, they present immense utility in understanding climate evolution throughout geologic history. Knowledge and understanding of the genesis of a soil is important in its classification and mapping. Soil classification systems cannot be based entirely on perceptions of genesis, however, because genetic processes are seldom observed and because pedogenic processes change over time. Knowledge of soil genesis is imperative and basic to soil use and management. Human influence on, or adjustment to, the factors and processes of soil formation can be best controlled and planned using knowledge about soil genesis. Soils are natural clay factories (clay includes both clay mineral structures and particles less than 2 µm in diameter). Shales worldwide are, to a considerable extent, simply soil clays that have been formed in the pedosphere and eroded and deposited in the ocean basins, to become lithified at a later date.

Sand

Sand is a naturally occurring granular material composed of finely divided rock and mineral particles.

As the term is used by geologists, sand particles range in diameter from 0.0625mm (or $^1/_{16}$ mm, or 62.5 micrometers) to 2 millimeters. An individual particle in this range size is termed a sand grain. The next larger size class above sand is gravel, with particles ranging from 2 mm up to 64 mm (see particle size for standards in use). The next smaller size class in geology is silt: particles smaller than 0.0625 mm down to 0.004 mm in diameter. The size specification between sand and gravel has remained constant for more than a century, but particle diameters as small as 0.02 mm were considered sand under the Albert Atterberg standard in use during the early 20th century. A 1953 engineering standard published by the American Association of State Highway and Transportation Officials set the minimum sand size at 0.074 mm. A 1938 specification of the United States Department of Agriculture was 0.05 mm. Sand feels gritty when rubbed between the fingers (silt, by comparison, feels like flour).

ISO 14688 grades sands as fine, medium and coarse with ranges 0.063 mm to 0.2 mm to 0.63 mm to 2.0 mm. In the United States, sand is commonly divided into five sub-categories based on size: very fine sand ($^1/_{16}$ - $^1/_8$ mm diameter), fine sand ($^1/_8$ mm - $^1/_4$ mm), medium sand ($^1/_4$ mm - $^1/_2$ mm), coarse sand ($^1/_2$ mm - 1 mm), and very coarse sand (1 mm - 2 mm). These sizes are based on the Krumbein phi scale, where size in F = -log base 2 of size in mm. On this scale, for sand the value of F varies from -1 to +4, with the divisions between sub-categories at whole numbers.

The most common constituent of sand, in inland continental settings and non-tropical coastal settings, is silica (silicon dioxide, or SiO_2), usually in the form of quartz, which, because of its chemical inertness and considerable hardness, is the most common mineral resistant to weathering.

The composition of sand is highly variable, depending on the local rock sources and conditions. The bright white sands found in tropical and subtropical coastal settings are eroded limestone and may contain coral and shell fragments in addition to other organic or organically derived fragmental material. The gypsum sand dunes of the White Sands National Monument in New Mexico are famous for their bright, white colour. Arkose is a sand or sandstone with considerable feldspar content, derived from the weathering and erosion of a (usually nearby) granitic rock outcrop. Some sands contain magnetite, chlorite, glauconite or gypsum. Sands rich in magnetite are dark to black in colour, as are sands derived from volcanic basalts and obsidian. Chlorite-glauconite bearing sands are typically green in colour, as are sands derived from basaltic (lava) with a high olivine content. Many sands, especially those found extensively in Southern Europe, have iron impurities within the quartz crystals of the sand, giving a deep yellow colour. Sand deposits in some areas contain garnets and other resistant minerals, including some small gemstones.

Environments

Sand is transported by wind and water and deposited in the form of beaches, dunes, sand spits, sand bars and related features. In environments such as gravel-bed rivers and glacial moraines it often occurs as one of the many grain sizes that are represented. Sand-bed rivers, such as the Platte River in Nebraska, USA, have sandy beds largely because there is no larger source material that they can transport. Dunes, on the other hand, are sandy because larger material is generally immobile in wind, and are a distinctive geographical feature of desert environments.The study of individual grains can reveal much historical information as to the origin and kind of transport of the grain. Quartz sand that is recently weathered from granite or gneiss quartz crystals will be angular. It is called grus in geology or sharp sand in the building trade where it is preferred for concrete, and in gardening where it is used as a soil amendment to loosen clay soils. Sand that is transported long distances by water or wind will be rounded, with characteristic abrasion patterns on the grain surface. Desert sand is typically rounded.

People who collect sand as a hobby are known as arenophiles or psammophiles.

Agriculture: Sandy soils are ideal for crops such as watermelons, peaches, and peanuts and their excellent drainage characteristics make them suitable for intensive dairy farming. Aquaria: Sand makes a low cost aquarium base material which some believe is better than gravel for home use. Artificial reefs: Geotextile bagged sand can serve as the foundation for new reefs. Beach nourishment: Governments move sand to beaches where tides, storms or deliberate changes to the shoreline erode the original sand. Brick: Manufacturing plants add sand to a mixture of clay and other materials for manufacturing bricks. Car Engine Disablement Sand is also used in addition to Sodium Silicate to inexpensively, quickly, and permanently disable automobile engines. Cob: Coarse sand makes up as much as 75 per cent of cob. Concrete: Sand is often a principal component of this critical construction material. Glass: Sand is the principal component in common glass. Landscaping: Sand makes small hills and slopes (for example, in golf courses). Paint: Mixing sand with paint produces a textured finish for walls and ceilings or non-slip floor surfaces. Railroads: Train operators use sand to improve the traction of wheels on the rails. Roads: Sand improves traction (and thus traffic safety) in icy or snowy conditions. Sand animation: Performance artists draw images in sand. Makers of animated films use the same term to describe their use of sand on frontlit or backlit glass. Sand casting: Casters moisten or oil molding sand, also known as foundry sand and then shape it into molds into which they pour molten material. This type of sand must be able to withstand high temperatures and pressure, allow gases to escape, have a uniform, small grain size and be non-reactive with metals. Sand castles: Shaping sand into castles or other miniature buildings is a popular beach activity. Sandbags: These protect against floods and gun fire. The inexpensive bags are easy to transport when empty, and unskilled volunteers can quickly fill them with local sand in emergencies.

Sandblasting: Graded sand serves as an abrasive in cleaning, preparing, and polishing. Water filtration: Media filters use sand for filtering water. Zoanthid 'skeletons': Animals in this order of marine benthic cnidarians related to corals and sea anemones, incorporate sand into their mesoglea for structural strength, which they need because they lack a true skeleton.

While sand is generally non-toxic, sand-using activities such as sandblasting require precautions. Bags of silica sand used for sandblasting now carry labels warning the user to wear respiratory protection to avoid breathing the resulting fine silica dust. Material safety data sheets (MSDS) for silica sand state that 'excessive inhalation of crystalline silica is a serious health concern'. In areas of high pore water pressure sand and salt water can form quicksand, which is a colloid hydrogel that behaves like a liquid. Quicksand produces a considerable barrier to escape for creatures caught within, who often die from exposure (not from submersion) as a result.

Environmental Issues

Sand's many uses require a significant dredging industry, raising environmental concerns over fish depletion, landslides, and flooding. Countries such as China, Indonesia, Malaysia and Cambodia ban sand exports, citing these issues as a major factor.

8 Erosion and Weathering

Erosion is a gravity driven process that moves solids (sediment, soil, rock and other particles) in the natural environment or their source and deposits them elsewhere. It usually occurs due to transport by wind, water, or ice; by down-slope creep of soil and other material under the force of gravity; or by living organisms, such as burrowing animals, in the case of bioerosion.

Erosion is a natural process, but it has been increased dramatically by human land use, especially industrial agriculture, deforestation, and urban sprawl. Land that is used for industrial agriculture generally experiences a significant greater rate of erosion than that of land under natural vegetation, or land used for sustainable agricultural practices. This is particularly true if tillage is used, which reduces vegetation cover on the surface of the soil and disturbs both soil structure and plant roots that would otherwise hold the soil in place. However, improved land use practices can limit erosion, using techniques such as terrace-building, conservation tillage practices, and tree planting.

A certain amount of erosion is natural and, in fact, healthy for the ecosystem. For example, gravels continuously move downstream in watercourses. Excessive erosion, however, causes serious problems, such as receiving water sedimentation, ecosystem damage and outright loss of soil.

Erosion is distinguished from weathering, which is the process of chemical or physical breakdown of the minerals in the rocks, although the two processes may occur concurrently.

The rate of erosion depends on many factors. Climatic factors include the amount and intensity of precipitation, the average temperature, as well as the typical temperature range, and seasonality, the wind speed, storm frequency. The geologic factors include the sediment or rock type, its porosity and permeability, the slope (gradient) of the land, and whether the rocks are tilted, faulted, folded, or weathered. The biological factors include ground cover from vegetation or lack thereof, the type of organisms inhabiting the area, and the land use.

In general, given similar vegetation and ecosystems, areas with high-intensity precipitation, more frequent rainfall, more wind, or more storms are expected to have more erosion. Sediment with high sand or silt contents and areas with steep slopes erode more easily, as do areas with highly fractured or weathered rock. Porosity and permeability of the sediment or rock affect the speed with which the water can percolate into the ground. If the water moves underground, less runoff is generated, reducing the amount of surface erosion. Sediments containing more clay tend to erode less than those with sand or silt. Here, however, the impact of atmospheric sodium on erodibility of clay should be considered.

The factor that is most subject to change is the amount and type of ground cover. In an undisturbed forest, the mineral soil is protected by a litter layer and an organic layer. These two layers protect the soil by absorbing the impact of rain drops. These layers and the underlying soil in a forest are porous and highly permeable to rainfall. Typically, only the most severe rainfall and large hailstorm events will lead to overland flow in a forest. If the trees are removed by fire or logging, infiltration rates become high and erosion low to the degree the forest floor remains intact. Severe fires can lead to significantly increased erosion if followed by heavy rainfall. In the case of construction or road building, when the litter layer is removed or compacted, the susceptibility of the soil to erosion is greatly increased.

Roads are especially likely to cause increased rates of erosion because, in addition to removing ground cover, they can significantly change drainage patterns, especially if an embankment has been made to support the road. A road that has a lot of rock and one that is 'hydrologically invisible' (that gets the water off the road as quickly as possible, mimicking natural drainage patterns) has the best chance of not causing increased erosion.

Many human activities remove vegetation from an area, making the soil easily eroded. Logging can cause increased erosion rates due to soil compaction, exposure of mineral soil, for example roads and landings. However it is the removal of or compromise to the forest floor not the removal of the canopy that can lead to erosion. This is because rain drops striking tree leaves coalesce with other rain drops creating larger drops. When these larger drops fall (called throughfall) they again may reach terminal velocity and strike the ground with more energy then had they fallen in the open. Terminal velocity of rain drops is reached in about 8 meters. Because forest canopies are usually higher than this, leaf drop can regain terminal velocity. However, the intact forest floor, with its layers of leaf litter and organic matter, absorbs the impact of the rainfall.

Heavy grazing can reduce vegetation enough to increase erosion. Changes in the kind of vegetation in an area can also affect erosion rates. Different kinds of vegetation lead to different infiltration rates of rain into the soil.

Forested areas have higher infiltration rates, so precipitation will result in less surface runoff, which erodes. Instead much of the water will go in subsurface flows, which are generally less erosive. Leaf litter and low shrubs are an important part of the high infiltration rates of forested systems, the removal of which can increase erosion rates. Leaf litter also shelters the soil from the impact of falling raindrops, which is a significant agent of erosion. Vegetation can also change the speed of surface runoff flows, so grasses and shrubs can also be instrumental in this aspect.

One of the main causes of erosive soil loss in the year 2006 is the result of slash and burn treatment of tropical forest. When the total ground surface is stripped of vegetation and then seared of all living organisms, the upper soils are vulnerable to both wind and water erosion. In a number of regions of the earth, entire sectors of a country have been rendered unproductive. For example, on the Madagascar high central plateau, comprising approximately ten per cent of that country's land area, virtually the entire landscape is sterile of vegetation, with gully erosive furrows typically in excess of 50 meters deep and one kilometer wide. Shifting cultivation is a farming system which sometimes incorporates the slash and burn method in some regions of the world. This degrades the soil and causes the soil to become less and less fertile.

Approximately 40 per cent of the world's agricultural land is seriously degraded. According to the UN, an area of fertile soil the size of Ukraine is lost every year because of drought, deforestation and climate change. In Africa, if current trends of soil degradation continue, the continent might be able to feed just 25 per cent of its population by 2025, according to UNU's Ghana-based Institute for Natural Resources in Africa.

When land is overused by animal activities (including humans), there can be mechanical erosion and also removal of vegetation leading to erosion. In the case of the animal kingdom, this effect would become material primarily with very large animal herds stampeding such as the Blue Wildebeest on the Serengeti plain. Even in this case there are broader material benefits to the ecosystem, such as continuing the survival of grasslands, that are indigenous to this region. This effect may be viewed as anomalous or a problem only when there is a significant imbalance or overpopulation of one species.

In the case of human use, the effects are also generally linked to overpopulation. When large number of hikers use trails or extensive off road vehicle use occurs, erosive effects often follow, arising from vegetation removal and furrowing of foot traffic and off road vehicle tires. These effects can also accumulate from a variety of outdoor human activities, again simply arising from too many people using a finite land resource.

One of the most serious and long-running water erosion problems worldwide is in the People's Republic of China, on the middle reaches of the Yellow River and the upper reaches of the Yangtze River. From the Yellow River, over 1.6 billion tons of sediment flows into the ocean each year. The sediment originates primarily from water erosion in the Loess Plateau region of the northwest.

Gravity

Mass wasting is the down-slope movement of rock and sediments, mainly due to the force of gravity. Mass movement is an important part of the erosional process, as it moves material from higher elevations to lower elevations where other eroding agents such as streams and glaciers can then pick up the material and move it to even lower elevations. Mass-movement processes are always occurring continuously on all slopes; some mass-movement processes act very slowly; others occur very suddenly, often with disastrous results. Any perceptible down-slope movement of rock or sediment is often referred to in general terms as a landslide. However, landslides can be classified in a much more detailed way that reflects the mechanisms responsible for the movement and the velocity at which the movement occurs. One of the visible topographical manifestations of a very slow form of such activity is a scree slope.

Slumping happens on steep hillsides, occurring along distinct fracture zones, often within materials like clay that, once released, may move quite rapidly downhill. They will often show a spoon-shaped isostatic depression, in which the material has begun to slide downhill. In some cases, the slump is caused by water beneath the slope weakening it. In many cases it is simply the result of poor engineering along highways where it is a regular occurrence.

Surface creep is the slow movement of soil and rock debris by gravity which is usually not perceptible except through extended observation. However, the term can also describe the rolling of dislodged soil particles 0.5 to 1.0 mm in diameter by wind along the soil surface.

Water

Splash erosion is the detachment and airborne movement of small soil particles caused by the impact of raindrops on soil.

Sheet erosion is the detachment of soil particles by raindrop impact and their removal downslope by water flowing overland as a sheet instead of in definite channels or rills. The impact of the raindrop breaks apart the soil aggregate. Particles of clay, silt and sand fill the soil pores and reduce infiltration. After the surface pores are filled with sand, silt or clay, overland surface flow of water begins due to the lowering of infiltration rates. Once the rate of falling rain is faster than infiltration, runoff takes place. There are two stages of sheet erosion. The first is rain splash, in which soil particles are knocked into the air by raindrop impact. In the second stage, the loose particles are moved downslope by broad sheets of rapidly flowing water filled with sediment known as sheetfloods. This stage of sheet erosion is generally produced by cloudbursts, sheetfloods commonly travel short distances and last only for a short time.

Rill erosion refers to the development of small, ephemeral concentrated flow paths, which function as both sediment source and sediment delivery systems for erosion on hillslopes. Generally, where water erosion rates on disturbed upland areas are greatest, rills are active. Flow depths in rills are typically on the order of a few centimeters or less and slopes may be quite steep. These conditions constitute a very different hydraulic environment than typically found in channels of streams and rivers. Eroding rills evolve morphologically in time and space. The rill bed surface changes as soil erodes, which in turn alters the hydraulics of the flow. The hydraulics is the driving mechanism for the erosion process, and therefore dynamically changing hydraulic patterns cause continually changing erosional patterns in the rill. Thus, the process of rill evolution involves a feedback loop between flow detachment, hydraulics, and bed form. Flow velocity, depth, width, hydraulic roughness, local bed slope, friction slope, and detachment rate are time and space variable functions of the rill evolutionary process. Superimposed on these interactive processes, the sediment load, or amount of sediment in the flow, has a large influence on soil detachment rates in rills. As sediment load increases, the ability of the flowing water to detach more sediment decreases.

Where precipitation rates exceed soil infiltration rates, *runoff* occurs. Surface runoff turbulence can often cause more erosion than the initial raindrop impact.

Gully erosion, also called *ephemeral gully erosion,* occurs when water flows in narrow channels during or immediately after heavy rains or melting snow. This is particularly noticeable in the formation of hollow ways, where, prior to being tarmacked, an old rural road has over many years become significantly lower than the surrounding fields.

A gully is sufficiently deep that it would not be routinely destroyed by tillage operations, whereas rill erosion is smoothed by ordinary farm tillage. The narrow channels, or gullies, may be of considerable depth, ranging from 1 to 2 feet to as much as 75 to 100 feet. Gully erosion is not accounted for in the revised universal soil loss equation.

Valley or *stream erosion* occurs with continued water flow along a linear feature. The erosion is both downward, deepening the valley, and headward, extending the valley into the hillside. In the earliest stage of stream erosion, the erosive activity is dominantly vertical, the valleys have a typical **V** cross-section and the stream gradient is relatively steep. When some base level is reached, the erosive activity switches to lateral erosion, which widens the valley floor and creates a narrow floodplain. The stream gradient becomes nearly flat, and lateral deposition of sediments becomes important as the stream meanders across the valley floor. In all stages of stream erosion, by far the most erosion occurs during times of flood, when more and faster-moving water is available to carry a larger sediment load. In such processes, it is not the water alone that erodes: suspended abrasive particles, pebbles and boulders can also act erosively as they traverse a surface.

At extremely high flows, kolks, or vortices are formed by large volumes of rapidly rushing water. Kolks cause extreme local erosion, plucking bedrock and creating pothole-type geographical features called Rock-cut basins. Examples can be seen in the flood regions result from glacial Lake Missoula, which created the channeled scablands in the Columbia Basin region of eastern Washington.

Shoreline erosion, which occurs on both exposed and sheltered coasts, primarily occurs through the action of currents and waves but sea level (tidal) change can also play a role.

Hydraulic action takes place when air in a joint is suddenly compressed by a wave closing the entrance of the joint. This then cracks it. *Wave pounding* is when the sheer energy of the wave hitting the cliff or rock breaks pieces off. *Abrasion* or *corrasion* is caused by waves launching seaload at the cliff. It is the most effective and rapid form of shoreline erosion (not to be confused with *corrosion*). *Corrosion* is the dissolving of rock by carbonic acid in sea water. Limestone cliffs are particularly vulnerable to this kind of erosion. *Attrition* is where particles/seaload carried by the waves are worn down as they hit each other and the cliffs. This then makes the material easier to wash away. The material ends up as shingle and sand. Another significant source of erosion, particularly on carbonate coastlines, is the boring, scraping and grinding of organisms, a process termed *bioerosion*.

Sediment is transported along the coast in the direction of the prevailing current (longshore drift). When the upcurrent amount of sediment is less than the amount being carried away, erosion occurs. When the upcurrent amount of sediment is greater, sand or gravel banks will tend to form. These banks may slowly migrate along the coast in the direction of the longshore drift, alternately protecting and exposing parts of the coastline. Where there is a bend in the coastline, quite often a build up of eroded material occurs forming a long narrow bank (a spit). Armoured beaches and submerged offshore sandbanks may also protect parts of a coastline from erosion. Over the years, as the shoals gradually shift, the erosion may be redirected to attack different parts of the shore.

Ice

Ice erosion can take one of two forms. It can be caused by the movement of ice, typically as glaciers, in a process called *glacial erosion*. It can also be due to freeze-thaw processes in which water inside pores and fractures in rock may expand cause further cracking.

Glaciers erode predominantly by three different processes: abrasion/scouring, plucking, and ice thrusting. In an abrasion process, debris in the basal ice scrapes along the bed, polishing and gouging the underlying rocks, similar to sandpaper on wood. Glaciers can also cause pieces of bedrock to crack off in the process of plucking. In ice thrusting, the glacier freezes to its bed, then as it surges forward, it moves large sheets of frozen sediment at the base along with the glacier. This method produced some of the many thousands of lake basins that dot the edge of the Canadian Shield. These processes, combined with erosion and transport by the water network beneath the glacier, leave moraines, drumlins, ground moraine (till), kames, kame deltas, moulins, and glacial erratics in their wake, typically at the terminus or during glacier retreat.

Cold weather causes water trapped in tiny rock cracks to freeze and expand, breaking the rock into several pieces. This can lead to gravity erosion on steep slopes. The scree which forms at the bottom of a steep mountainside is mostly formed from pieces of rock (soil) broken away by this means. It is a common engineering problem wherever rock cliffs are alongside roads, because morning thaws can drop hazardous rock pieces onto the road.

In some places, water seeps into rocks during the daytime, then freezes at night. Ice expands, thus, creating a wedge in the rock. Over time, the repetition in the forming and melting of the ice causes fissures, which eventually breaks the rock down.

Wind

In arid climates, the main source of erosion is wind. The general wind circulation moves small particulates such as dust across wide oceans thousands of kilometers downwind of their point of origin, which is known as deflation. Erosion can be the result of material movement by the wind. There are two main effects. First, wind causes small particles to be lifted and therefore moved to another region. This is called deflation. Second, these suspended particles may impact on solid objects causing erosion by abrasion (ecological succession). Wind erosion generally occurs in areas with little or no vegetation, often in areas where there is insufficient rainfall to support vegetation. An example is the formation of sand dunes, on a beach or in a desert. Loess is a homogeneous, typically non-stratified, porous, friable, slightly coherent, often calcareous, fine-grained, silty, pale yellow or buff, windblown (aeolian) sediment. It generally occurs as a widespread blanket deposit that covers areas of hundreds of square kilometers and tens of meters thick. Loess often stands in either steep or vertical faces. Loess tends to develop into highly rich soils. Under appropriate climatic conditions, areas with loess are among the most agriculturally productive in the world. Loess deposits are geologically unstable by nature, and will erode very readily. Therefore, windbreaks (such as big trees and bushes) are often planted by farmers to reduce the wind erosion of loess.

Thermal

Thermal erosion is the result of melting and weakening permafrost due to moving water It can occur both along rivers and at the coast. Rapid river channel migration observed in the Lena River of Siberia is due to thermal erosion, as these portions of the banks are composed of permafrost-cemented non-cohesive materials. Much of this erosion occurs as the weakened banks fail in large slumps. Thermal erosion also affects the Arctic coast, where wave action and near-shore temperatures combine to undercut permafrost bluffs along the shoreline and cause them to fail. Annual erosion rates along a 100-kilometer segment of the Beaufort Sea shoreline averaged 5.6 meters per year from 1955 to 2002.

Soil Erosion and Climate Change

The warmer atmospheric temperatures observed over the past decades are expected to lead to a more vigorous hydrological cycle, including more extreme rainfall events.

In 1998 Karl and Knight reported that from 1910 to 1996 total precipitation over the contiguous U.S. increased, and that 53 per cent of the increase came from the upper 10 per cent of precipitation events (the most intense precipitation). The percent of precipitation coming from days of precipitation in excess of 50 mm has also increased significantly.

Studies on soil erosion suggest that increased rainfall amounts and intensities will lead to greater rates of erosion. Thus, if rainfall amounts and intensities increase in many parts of the world as expected, erosion will also increase, unless amelioration measures are taken. Soil erosion rates are expected to change in response to changes in climate for a variety of reasons. The most direct is the change in the erosive power of rainfall. Other reasons include:

(a) changes in plant canopy caused by shifts in plant biomass production associated with moisture regime;

(b) changes in litter cover on the ground caused by changes in both plant residue decomposition rates driven by temperature and moisture dependent soil microbial activity as well as plant biomass production rates;

(c) changes in soil moisture due to shifting precipitation regimes and evapo-transpiration rates, which changes infiltration and runoff ratios;

(d) soil erodibility changes due to decrease in soil organic matter concentrations in soils that lead to a soil structure that is more susceptible to erosion and increased runoff due to increased soil surface sealing and crusting;

(e) a shift of winter precipitation from non-erosive snow to erosive rainfall due to increasing winter temperatures;

(f) melting of permafrost, which induces an erodible soil state from a previously non-erodible one; and

(g) shifts in land use made necessary to accommodate new climatic regimes.

Studies by Pruski and Nearing indicated that, other factors such as land use not considered, we can expect approximately a 1.7 per cent change in soil erosion for each 1 per cent change in total precipitation under climate change.

Tectonic Effects

The removal by erosion of large amounts of rock from a particular region, and its deposition elsewhere, can result in a lightening of the load on the lower crust and mantle. This can cause tectonic or isostatic uplift in the region. Research undertaken since the early 1990s suggests that the spatial distribution of erosion at the surface of an orogen can exert a key influence on its growth and its final internal structure.

Materials Science

In materials science, erosion is the recession of surfaces by repeated localized mechanical trauma as, for example, by suspended abrasive particles within a moving fluid. Erosion can also occur from non-abrasive fluid mixtures. Cavitation is one example.

In hard particle erosion, the hardness of the impacted material is a large factor in the mechanics of the erosion. A soft material will typically erode fastest from glancing impacts. Harder material will typically erode fastest from perpendicular impacts. Hardness is a correlative factor for erosion resistance, but a higher hardness does not guarantee better resistance. Factors that affect the erosion rate also include impacting particle speed, size, density, hardness, and rotation. Coatings can be applied to retard erosion, but normally can only slow the removal of material. Erosion rate for solid particle impact is typically measured as mass of material removed divided by the mass of impacting material.

The concept of erosion is commonly employed by analogy to various forms of perceived or real homogenization (*i.e.* erosion of boundaries), 'leveling out', collusion or even the decline of anything from morals to indigenous cultures. It is a common trope of the English language to describe as *erosion* the gradual, organic mutation of something thought of as distinct, more complex, harder to pronounce or more refined into something indistinct, less complex, easier to pronounce or (disparagingly) less refined.

Weathering

Weathering is the breaking down of Earth's rocks, soils and minerals through direct contact with the planet's atmosphere. Weathering occurs *in situ*, or 'with no movement', and thus should not be confused with erosion, which involves the movement of rocks and minerals by agents such as water, ice, wind and gravity.

Two important classifications of weathering processes exist – physical and chemical weathering. *Mechanical* or *physical weathering* involves the breakdown of rocks and soils through direct contact with atmospheric conditions, such as heat, water, ice and pressure. The second classification, *chemical weathering,* involves the direct effect of atmospheric chemicals or biologically produced chemicals (also known as *biological weathering*) in the breakdown of rocks, soils and minerals.

The materials left over after the rock breaks down combined with organic material creates soil. The mineral content of the soil is determined by the parent material, thus a soil derived from a single rock type can often be deficient in one or more minerals for good fertility, while a soil weathered from a mix of rock types (as in glacial, aeolian or alluvial sediments) often makes more fertile soil.

Physical Weathering

Physical weathering is the only process that causes the disintegration of rocks without chemically changing it. The primary process in physical weathering is abrasion (the process by which clasts and other particles are reduced in size). However, chemical and physical weathering often go hand in hand. For example, cracks exploited by physical weathering will increase the surface area exposed to chemical action. Furthermore, the chemical action at minerals in cracks can aid the disintegration process.

Thermal Expansion

Thermal expansion, also known as exfoliation, insolation weathering or thermal shock, often occurs in areas, like deserts, where there is a large diurnal temperature range. The temperatures soar high in the day, while dipping greatly at night. As the rock heats up and expands by day, and cools and contracts by night, stress is often exerted on the outer layers. The stress causes the peeling off of the outer layers of rocks in thin sheets. Though this is caused mainly by temperature changes, thermal expansion is enhanced by the presence of moisture. Forest fires and range fires are also known to cause significant weathering of rocks and boulders exposed along the ground surface. Intense, localized heat can rapidly expand a boulder, causing its surface to exfoliate or spall. The weathering process was evident especially after the massive wildfires in Wyoming that occurred in 1988.

Frost Disintegration

This process can also be called frost shattering, frost-wedging or freeze-thaw weathering. This type of weathering is common in mountain areas where the temperature is around the freezing point of water. Moist soils expand or frost heave upon freezing as a result of water migrating along from unfrozen areas via thin films to collect at growing ice lenses. This same phenomena occurs within pore spaces of rocks. The ice accumulations grow larger as they attract liquid water from the surrounding pores. The ice crystal growth weakens the rocks which, in time, break up. It is caused by the expansion of ice when water freezes, so putting considerable stress on the walls of containment. The same process acts on roads, creating potholes after the thaw.

Freeze induced weathering action occurs mainly in environments where there is a lot of moisture, and temperatures frequently fluctuate above and below freezing point—that is, mainly alpine and periglacial areas. An example of rocks susceptible to frost action is chalk, which has many pore spaces for the growth of ice crystals. This process can be seen in Dartmoor where it results in the formation of tors. When water that has entered the joints freezes, the ice formed strains the walls of the joints and causes the joints to deepen and widen. When the ice thaws, water can flow further into the rock. Repeated freeze-thaw cycles weaken the rocks which, over time, break up along the joints into angular pieces. The angular rock fragments gather at the foot of the slope to form a talus slope (or scree slope). The splitting of rocks along the joints into blocks is called block disintegration. The blocks of rocks that are detached are of various shapes depending on rock structure.

Pressure Release

In pressure release, also known as unloading, overlying materials (not necessarily rocks) are removed (by erosion, or other processes), which causes underlying rocks to expand and fracture parallel to the surface. Often the overlying material is heavy, and the underlying rocks experience high pressure under them, for example, a moving glacier. Pressure release may also cause exfoliation to occur.

Intrusive igneous rocks (*e.g.* granite) are formed deep beneath the Earth's surface. They are under tremendous pressure because of the overlying rock material. When erosion removes the overlying rock material, these intrusive rocks are exposed and the pressure on them is released. The outer parts of the rocks then tend to expand. The expansion sets up stresses which cause fractures parallel to the rock surface to form. Over time, sheets of rock break away from the exposed rocks along the fractures. Pressure release is also known as 'exfoliation' or 'sheeting'; these processes result in batholiths and granite domes, an example of which is Dartmoor.

Hydraulic Action

This is when water (generally from powerful waves) rushes into cracks in the rockface rapidly. This traps a layer of air at the bottom of the crack, compressing it and weakening the rock. When the wave retreats, the trapped air is suddenly released with explosive force. The explosive release of highly pressurized air cracks away fragments at the rockface and widens the crack itself.

Salt-crystal Growth (Haloclasty)

Salt crystallization, otherwise known as haloclasty, causes disintegration of rocks when saline (see salinity) solutions seep into cracks and joints in the rocks and evaporate, leaving salt crystals behind. These salt crystals expand as they are heated up, exerting pressure on the confining rock.

Salt crystallization may also take place when solutions decompose rocks (for example, limestone and chalk) to form salt solutions of sodium sulfate or sodium carbonate, of which the moisture evaporates to form their respective salt crystals.

The salts which have proved most effective in disintegrating rocks are sodium sulfate, magnesium sulfate, and calcium chloride. Some of these salts can expand up to three times or even more.

It is normally associated with arid climates where strong heating causes strong evaporation and therefore salt crystallization. It is also common along coasts. An example of salt weathering can be seen in the honeycombed stones in sea wall. Honeycomb is a type of tafoni, a class of cavernous rock weathering structures, which likely develop in large part by chemical and physical salt weathering processes.

Biological Weathering

Living organisms may contribute to mechanical weathering (as well as chemical weathering, see 'biological' weathering below). Lichens and mosses grow on essentially bare rock surfaces and create a more humid chemical microenvironment. The attachment of these organisms to the rock surface enhances physical as well as chemical breakdown of the surface microlayer of the rock. On a larger scale seedlings sprouting in a crevice and plant roots exert physical pressure as well as providing a pathway for water and chemical infiltration. Burrowing animals and insects disturb the soil layer adjacent to the bedrock surface thus further increasing water and acid infiltration and exposure to oxidation processes.

Chemical weathering involves the change in the composition of rocks, often leading to a 'break down' in its form. This is done through a combination of water and various chemicals to create an acid which directly breaks down the material.

Chemical weathering is a gradual and ongoing process as the mineralogy of the rock adjusts to the near surface environment. New or *secondary minerals* develop from the original minerals of the rock. In this the processes of oxidation and hydrolysis are most important.

Dissolution

Rainfall is acidic because atmospheric carbon dioxide dissolves in the rainwater producing weak carbonic acid. In unpolluted environments, the rainfall pH is around 5.6. Acid rain occurs when gases such as sulphur dioxide and nitrogen oxides are present in the atmosphere. These oxides react in the rain water to produce stronger acids and can lower the pH to 4.5 or even 3.0. Sulfur dioxide, SO_2, comes from volcanic eruptions or from fossil fuels, can become sulfuric acid within rainwater, which can cause solution weathering to the rocks on which it falls.

One of the most well-known solution weathering processes is carbonation, the process in which atmospheric carbon dioxide leads to solution weathering. Carbonation occurs on rocks which contain calcium carbonate, such as limestone and chalk. This takes place when rain combines with carbon dioxide or an organic acid to form a weak carbonic acid which reacts with calcium carbonate (the limestone) and forms calcium bicarbonate. This process speeds up with a decrease in temperature, not because low temperatures generally drive reactions faster, but because colder water holds more dissolved carbon dioxide gas. Carbonation is therefore is a large feature of glacial weathering.

The reactions as follows:

$CO_2 + H_2O \Rightarrow H_2CO_3$

carbon dioxide + water ⇒ carbonic acid

$H_2CO_3 + CaCO_3 \Rightarrow Ca(HCO_3)_2$

carbonic acid + calcium carbonate ⇒ calcium bicarbonate

Carbonation on the surface of well-jointed limestone produces a dissected limestone pavement which is most effective along the joints, widening and deepening them.

Hydration

Mineral hydration is a form of chemical weathering that involves the rigid attachment of H+ and OH- ions to the atoms and molecules of a mineral.

When rock minerals take up water, the increased volume creates physical stresses within the rock. For example iron oxides are converted to iron hydroxides and the hydration of anhydrite forms gypsum.

This hydrolysis reaction is much more common. Carbonic acid is consumed by silicate weathering, resulting in more alkaline solutions because of the bicarbonate. This is an important reaction in controlling the amount of CO_2 in the atmosphere and can affect climate.

Aluminosilicates when subjected to the hydrolysis reaction produce a secondary mineral rather than simply releasing cations.

Oxidation

Within the weathering environment chemical oxidation of a variety of metals occurs. The most commonly observed is the oxidation of Fe^{2+} (iron) and combination with oxygen and water to form Fe^{3+} hydroxides and oxides such as goethite, limonite, and hematite. This gives the affected rocks a reddish-brown coloration on the surface which crumbles easily and weakens the rock. This process is better known as 'rusting'. Many other metallic ores and minerals oxidize and hydrate to produce coloured deposits, such as chalcopyrites or $CuFeS_2$ oxidizing to copper hydroxide and iron oxides.

Biological

A number of plants and animals may create chemical weathering through release of acidic compounds, *i.e* moss on roofs is classed as weathering.

The most common form of biological weathering is the release of chelating compounds, *i.e* acids, by plants so as to break down aluminium and iron containing compounds in the soils beneath them. Decaying remains of dead plants in soil may form organic acids which, when dissolved in water, cause chemical weathering. Extreme release of chelating compounds can easily affect surrounding rocks and soils, and may lead to podsolisation of soils.

Building Weathering

Buildings made of any stone, brick or concrete are susceptible to the same weathering agents as any exposed rock surface. Also statues, monuments and ornamental stonework can be badly damaged by natural weathering processes. This is accelerated in areas severely affected by acid rain.

9 Clay

Clay is a naturally occurring material composed primarily of fine-grained minerals, which show plasticity through a variable range of water content, and which can be hardened when dried and/or fired. Clay deposits are mostly composed of clay minerals (phyllosilicate minerals), minerals which impart plasticity and harden when fired and/or dried, and variable amounts of water trapped in the mineral structure by polar attraction. Organic materials which do not impart plasticity may also be a part of clay deposits.

Formation

Clay minerals are typically formed over long periods of time by the gradual chemical weathering of rocks, usually silicate-bearing, by low concentrations of carbonic acid and other diluted solvents. These solvents, usually acidic, migrate through the weathering rock after leaching through upper weathered layers. In addition to the weathering process, some clay minerals are formed by hydrothermal activity. Clay deposits may be formed in place as residual deposits in soil, but thick deposits usually are formed as the result of a secondary sedimentary deposition process after they have been eroded and transported from their original location of formation. Clay deposits are typically associated with very low energy depositional environments such as large lakes and marine deposits.

Primary clays, also known as kaolins, are located at the site of formation. Secondary clay deposits have been moved by erosion and water from their primary location.

Definition

Clays are distinguished from other fine-grained soils by differences in size and/or mineralogy. Silts, which are fine-grained soils which do not include clay minerals, tend to have larger particle sizes than clays, but there is some overlap in both particle size and other physical properties, and there are many naturally occurring deposits which include both silts and clays. The distinction between silt and clay varies by discipline. Geologists and soil scientists usually consider the separation to occur at a particle size of 2 μm (clays being finer than silts), sedimentologists often use 4-5 μm, and colloid chemists use 1 μm. Geotechnical engineers distinguish between silts and clays based on the plasticity properties of the soil, as measured by the soils' Atterberg Limits. ISO 14688 grades clay particles as being smaller than 2 μm and silts larger.

Grouping

Depending on the academic source, there are three or four main groups of clays: kaolinite, montmorillonite-smectite, illite and chlorite. Chlorites are not always considered a clay, sometimes being classified as a separate group within the phyllosilicates. There are approximately 30 different types of 'pure' clays in these categories, but most 'natural' clays are mixtures of these different types, along with other weathered minerals.

Varve (or *varved clay*) is clay with visible annual layers, formed by seasonal differences in erosion and organic content. This type of deposit is common in former glacial lakes. When glacial lakes are formed there is very little movement of the water that makes the lake, and these eroded soils settle on the lake bed. This allows such an even distribution on the different layers of clay.

Quick clay is a unique type of marine clay indigenous to the glaciated terrains of Norway, Canada, Northern Ireland and Sweden. It is a highly sensitive clay, prone to liquefaction, which has been involved in several deadly landslides.

Historical and Modern Uses

Clays exhibit plasticity when mixed with water in certain proportions. When dry, clay becomes firm and when fired in a kiln, permanent physical and chemical reactions occur. These reactions, among other changes, cause the clay to be converted into a ceramic material. Because of these properties, clay is used for making pottery items, both utilitarian and decorative. Different types of clay, when used with different minerals and firing conditions, are used to produce earthenware, stoneware and porcelain. Prehistoric humans discovered the useful properties of clay, and one of the earliest artifacts ever uncovered is a drinking vessel made of sun-dried clay. Depending on the content of the soil, clay can appear in various colours, from a dull gray to a deep orange-red.

Clay tablets were used as the first writing medium, inscribed with cuneiform script through the use of a blunt reed called a stylus.

Clays sintered in fire were the first form of ceramic. Bricks, cooking pots, art objects, dishware and even musical instruments such as the ocarina can all be shaped from clay before being fired. Clay is also used in many industrial processes, such as paper making, cement production and chemical filtering. Clay is also often used in the manufacture of pipes for smoking tobacco. Until the late 20th century bentonite clay was widely used as a mold binder in the manufacture of sand castings.

Clay, being relatively impermeable to water, is also used where natural seals are needed, such as in the cores of dams, or as a barrier in landfills against toxic seepage ('lining' the landfill, preferably in combination with geotextiles).

Recent studies have investigated clay's absorption capacities in various applications, such as the removal of heavy metals from waste water and air purification.

Medical and Agricultural Uses

A traditional use of clay, such as Armenian bole, is to soothe an upset stomach, similar to the way parrots (and later, humans) in South America originally used it.

A more recent, and more limited, use is as a specially formulated spray applied to fruits, vegetables and other vegetation to repel or deter codling moth damage, and at least for apples, to prevent sun scald.

A recent article in *The Journal of Antimicrobial Chemotherapy* found that certain iron-rich clay was effective in killing bacteria.

10 Soil Contamination

Soil pollution is caused by the presence of xenobiotic (man-made) chemicals or other alteration in the natural soil environment. This type of contamination typically arises from the rupture of underground storage tanks, application of pesticides, percolation of contaminated surface water to subsurface strata, oil and fuel dumping, leaching of wastes from landfills or direct discharge of industrial wastes to the soil. The most common chemicals involved are petroleum hydrocarbons, solvents, pesticides, lead and other heavy metals. This occurrence of this phenomenon is correlated with the degree of industrializations and intensities of chemical usage.The concern over soil contamination stems primarily from health risks, from direct contact with the contaminated soil, vapours from the contaminants, and from secondary contamination of water supplies within and underlying the soil. Mapping of contaminated soil sites and the resulting clean-up are time consuming and expensive tasks, requiring extensive amounts of geology, hydrology, chemistry and computer modelling skills. It is in North America and Western Europe that the extent of contaminated land is most well known, with many of countries in these areas having a legal framework to identify and deal with this environmental problem; this however may well be just the tip of the iceberg with developing countries very likely to be the next generation of new soil contamination cases.The immense and sustained growth of the People's Republic of China since the 1970s has exacted a price from the land in increased soil pollution. The State Environmental Protection Administration believes it to be a threat to the environment, to food safety and to sustainable agriculture. According to a scientific sampling, 150 million mi (100,000 square kilometres) of China's cultivated land have been polluted, with contaminated water being used to irrigate a further 32.5 million mi (21,670 square kilometres) and another 2 million mi (1,300 square kilometres) covered or destroyed by solid waste. In total, the area accounts for one-tenth of China's cultivatable land, and is mostly in economically developed areas. An estimated 12 million tonnes of grain are contaminated by heavy metals every year, causing direct losses of 20 billion yuan (US$2.57 billion).

The United States, while having some of the most widespread soil contamination, has actually been a leader in defining and implementing standards for clean-up. Other industrialized countries have a large number of contaminated sites, but lag the U.S. in executing remediation. Developing countries may be leading in the next generation of new soil contamination cases.

Each year in the U.S., thousands of sites complete soil contamination clean-up, some by using microbes that 'eat up' toxic chemicals in soil, many others by simple excavation and others by more expensive high-tech soil vapor extraction or air stripping. Efforts proceed worldwide to identify new sites of soil contamination.

Health Effects

Contaminated soil directly affects human health through direct contact with soil or via inhalation of soil contaminants which have vaporized; potentially greater threats are posed by the infiltration of soil contamination into groundwater aquifers used for human consumption, sometimes in areas apparently far removed from any apparent source of above ground contamination.

Health consequences from exposure to soil contamination vary greatly depending on pollutant type, pathway of attack and vulnerability of the exposed population. Chronic exposure to chromium, lead and other metals, petroleum, solvents, and many pesticide and herbicide formulations can be carcinogenic, can cause congenital disorders, or can cause other chronic health conditions. Anthropomorphic concentrations of naturally-occurring substances such as nitrate and ammonia associated with livestock manure from agricultural operations, have also been identified as health hazards in soil and groundwater.

Chronic exposure to benzene at sufficient concentrations is known to be associated with higher incidence of leukemia. Mercury and cyclodienes are known to induce higher incidences of kidney damage, some irreversible. PCBs and cyclodienes are linked to liver toxicity. Organophosphates and carbamates can induce a chain of responses leading to neuromuscular blockage. Many chlorinated solvents induce liver changes, kidney changes and depression of the central nervous system. There is an entire spectrum of further health effects such as headache, nausea, fatigue, eye irritation and skin rash for the above cited and other chemicals. At sufficient dosages a large number of soil contaminants can cause death by exposure via direct contact, inhalation or ingestion of contaminants in groundwater contaminated through soil.

Ecosystem Effects

Not unexpectedly, soil contaminants can have significant deleterious consequences for ecosystems . There are radical soil chemistry changes which can arise from the presence of many hazardous chemicals even at low concentration of the contaminant species. These changes can manifest in the alteration of metabolism of endemic microorganisms and arthropods resident in a given soil environment. The result can be virtual eradication of some of the primary food chain, which in turn have major consequences for predator or consumer species. Even if the chemical effect on lower life forms is small, the lower pyramid levels of the food chain may ingest alien chemicals, which normally become more concentrated for each consuming rung of the food chain. Many of these effects are now well known, such as the concentration of persistent DDT materials for avian consumers, leading to weakening of egg shells, increased chick mortality and potential extinction of species.

Effects occur to agricultural lands which have certain types of soil contamination. Contaminants typically alter plant metabolism, most commonly to reduce crop yields. This has a secondary effect upon soil conservation, since the languishing crops cannot shield the Earth's soil mantle from erosion phenomena. Some of these chemical contaminants have long half-lives and in other cases derivative chemicals are formed from decay of primary soil contaminants.

REGULATORY FRAMEWORK

United States of America

Until about 1970 there was little widespread awareness of the worldwide scope of soil contamination or its health risks. In fact, areas of concern were often viewed as unusual or isolated incidents. Since then, the U.S. has established guidelines for handling hazardous waste and the cleanup of soil pollution. In 1980 the U.S.Superfund/CERCLA established strict rules on legal liability for soil contamination. Not only did CERCLA stimulate identification and cleanup of thousands of sites, but it raised awareness of property buyers and sellers to make soil pollution a focal issue of land use and management practices.

While estimates of remaining soil clean-up in the U.S. may exceed 2,00,000 sites, hundreds of new sites are identified each year, and in other industrialized countries there is a lag of identification and cleanup functions. Even though their use of chemicals is lower than industrialized countries, often their controls and regulatory framework is quite weak. For example, some persistent pesticides that have been banned in the U.S. are in widespread uncontrolled use in developing countries. It is worth noting that the cost of cleaning up a soil contaminated site can range from as little as about $10,000 for a small spill, which can be simply excavated, to millions of dollars for a widespread event, especially for a chemical that is very mobile such as perchloroethylene.

United Kingdom

Generic guidance commonly used in the UK are the Soil Guideline Values published by DEFRA and the Environment Agency. These are screening values that demonstrate the minimal acceptable level of a substance. Above this there can be no assurances in terms of significant risk of harm to human health. These have been derived using the Contaminated Land Exposure Assessment Model (CLEA UK). Certain input parameters such as Health Criteria Values, age and land use are fed into CLEA UK to obtain a probabilistic output.

Guidance by the Inter Departmental Committee for the Redevelopment of Contaminated Land (ICRCL) has been formally withdrawn by the Department for Environment, Food and Rural Affairs (DEFRA), for use as a prescriptive document to determine the potential need for remediation or further assessment. Therefore, no further reference is made to these former guideline values.

Other generic guidance that exists (to put the concentration of a particular contaminant in context), includes the United States EPA Region 9 Preliminary Remediation Goals (US PRGs), the US EPA Region 3 Risk Based Concentrations (US EPA RBCs) and National Environment Protection Council of Australia Guideline on Investigation Levels in Soil and Groundwater.

However international guidance should only be used in the UK with clear justification. This is because foreign standards are usually particular to that country due to drivers such as political policy, geology, flood regime and epidemiology. It is generally accepted by UK regulators that only robust scientific methods that relate to the UK should be used.

The CLEA model published by DEFRA and the Environment Agency (EA) in March 2002 sets a framework for the appropriate assessment of risks to human health from contaminated land, as required by Part IIA of the Environmental Protection Act 1990. As part of this framework, generic Soil Guideline Values (SGVs) have currently been derived for ten contaminants to be used as 'intervention values'. These values should not be considered as remedial targets but values above which further detailed assessment should be considered.

Three sets of CLEA SGVs have been produced for three different land uses, namely:

- residential (with and without plant uptake);
- allotments; and
- commercial/industrial.

It is intended that the SGVs replace the former ICRCL values. It should be noted that the CLEA SGVs relate to assessing chronic (long term) risks to human health and do not apply to the protection of ground workers during construction, or other potential receptors such as groundwater, buildings, plants or other ecosystems. The CLEA SGVs are not directly applicable to a site completely covered in hardstanding, as there is no direct exposure route to contaminated soils.

To date, the first ten of fifty-five contaminant SGVs have been published, for the following: arsenic, cadmium, chromium, lead, inorganic mercury, nickel, selenium ethyl benzene, phenol and toluene. Draft SGVs for benzene, naphthalene and xylene have been produced but their publication is on hold. Toxicological data (Tox) has been published for each of these contaminants as well as for benzo[a]pyrene, benzene, dioxins, furans and dioxin-like PCBs, naphthalene, vinyl chloride, 1, 1, 2, 2 tetrachloroethane and 1, 1, 1, 2 tetrachloroethane, 1, 1, 1 trichloroethane, tetrachloroethene, carbon tetrachloride, 1, 2-dichloroethane, trichloroethene and xylene. The SGVs for ethyl benzene, phenol and toluene are dependent on the soil organic matter (SOM) content (which can be calculated from the total organic carbon (TOC) content). As an initial screen the SGVs for 1 per cent SOM are considered to be appropriate.

Clean-up Options

Clean-up or remediation is analyzed by environmental scientists who utilize field measurement of soil chemicals and also apply computer models for analyzing transport and fate of soil chemicals. Thousands of soil contamination cases are currently in active clean-up across the U.S. as of 2006. There are several principal strategies for remediation:

- Excavate soil and take it to a disposal site away from ready pathways for human or sensitive ecosystem contact. This technique also applies to dredging of bay muds containing toxins.
- Aeration of soils at the contaminated site (with attendant risk of creating air pollution)
- Thermal remediation by introduction of heat to raise subsurface temperatures sufficiently high to volatize chemical contaminants out of the soil for vapour extraction. Technologies include ISTD, electrical resistance heating (ERH), and ET-DSP^{tm}.

Bioremediation, involving microbial digestion of certain organic chemicals. Techniques used in bioremediation include landfarming, biostimulation and bioaugmentating soil biota with commercially available microflora. Extraction of groundwater or soil vapour with an active electromechanical system, with subsequent stripping of the contaminants from the extract. Containment of the soil contaminants (such as by capping or paving over in place). Phytoremediation, or using plants (such as willow) to extract heavy metals.

11 Soil Conservation

Soil conservation is a set of management strategies for prevention of soil being eroded from the earth's surface or becoming chemically altered by overuse, acidification, salinization or other chemical soil contamination. The principle approaches these strategies take are:

- sheep pasture with macroscale erosion, Australia;
- choice of vegetative cover;
- erosion prevention;
- salinity management;
- acidity control;
- encouraging health of beneficial soil organisms;
- prevention and remediation of soil contamination; and
- mineralization.

Other ways are:

- no till farming;
- contour plowing;
- wind rows;
- crop rotation;

- the use of natural and man-made fertilizer; and
- resting the land (Shmita). Many scientific disciplines are involved in these pursuits, including agronomy, hydrology, soil science, meteorology, microbiology, and environmental chemistry.

Decisions regarding appropriate crop rotation, cover crops, and planted windbreaks are central to the ability of surface soils to retain their integrity, both with respect to erosive forces and chemical change from nutrient depletion. Crop rotation is simply the conventional alternation of crops on a given field, so that nutrient depletion is avoided from repetitive chemical uptake/deposition of single crop growth.

Cover crops serve the function of protecting the soil from erosion, weed establishment or excess evapotranspiration; however, they may also serve vital soil chemistry functions . For example, legumes can be ploughed under to augment soil nitrates, and other plants have the ability to metabolize soil contaminants or alter adverse pH. The cover crop Mucuna pruriens (velvet bean) has been used in Nigeria to increase phosphorus availability after application of rock phosphate . Some of these same precepts are applicable to urban landscaping, especially with respect to ground-cover selection for erosion control and weed suppression.

Windbreaks are created by planting sufficiently dense rows or stands of trees at the windward exposure of an agricultural field subject to wind erosion . Evergreen species are preferred to achieve year-round protection; however, as long as foliage is present in the seasons of bare soil surfaces, the effect of deciduous trees may also be adequate. Trees, shrubs and groundcovers are also effective perimeter treatment for soil erosion prevention, by insuring any surface flows are impeded. A special form of this perimeter or inter-row treatment is the use of a 'grassway' that both channels and dissipates runoff through surface friction, impeding surface runoff, and encouraging infiltration of the slowed surface water.

Erosion Prevention

There are also conventional practices that farmers have invoked for centuries. These fall into two main categories: contour farming and terracing, standard methods recommended by the U.S. Natural Resources Conservation Service, whose Code 330 is the common standard. Contour farming was practiced by the ancient Phoenicians, and is known to be effective for slopes between two and ten per cent. Contour plowing can increase crop yields from 10 to 50 per cent, partially as a result from greater soil retention.

There are many erosion control methods that can be used such as conservation tillage systems and crop rotation.

Keyline design is an enhancement of contour farming, where the total watershed properties are taken into account in forming the contour lines. Terracing is the practice of creating benches or nearly level layers on a hillside setting. Terraced farming is more common on small farms and in underdeveloped countries, since mechanized equipment is difficult to deploy in this setting.

Human overpopulation is leading to destruction of tropical forests due to widening practices of slash-and-burn and other methods of subsistence farming necessitated by famines in lesser developed countries. A sequel to the deforestation is typically large scale erosion, loss of soil nutrients and sometimes total desertification.

Salinity Management

The ions responsible for salination are: Na^+, K^+, Ca^{2+}, Mg^{2+} and Cl^-. Salinity is estimated to affect about one third of all the earth's arable land. Soil salinity adversely affects the metabolism of most crops, and erosion effects usually follow vegetation failure. Salinity occurs on drylands from overirrigation and in areas with shallow saline water tables. In the case of over-irrigation, salts are deposited in upper soil layers as a byproduct of most soil infiltration; excessive irrigation merely increases the rate of salt deposition. The best-known case of shallow saline water table capillary action occurred in Egypt after the 1970 construction of the Aswan Dam. The change in the groundwater level due to dam construction led to high concentration of salts in the water table. After the construction, the continuous high level of the water table led to soil salination of previously arable land.

Use of humic acids may prevent excess salination, especially in locales where excessive irrigation was practiced. The mechanism involved is that humic acids can fix both anions and cations and eliminate them from root zones. In some cases it may be valuable to find plants that can tolerate saline conditions to use as surface cover until salinity can be reduced; there are a number of such saline-tolerant plants, such as saltbush, a plant found in much of North America and in the Mediterranean regions of Europe.

Soil Per Cent Hydrogen (pH)

Soil pH levels in Lake Titikaka tend to crop growth can occur naturally in some regions; it can also be induced by acid rain or soil contamination from acids or bases. The role of soil pH is to control nutrient availability to vegetation. The principal macronutrients (calcium, phosphorus, nitrogen, potassium, magnesium, sulfur) prefer neutral to slightly alkaline soils. Calcium, magnesium and potassium are usually made available to plants via cation exchange surfaces of organic material and clay soil surface particles. While acidification increases the initial availability of these cations, the residual soil moisture concentrations of nutrient cations can fall to alarmingly low levels after initial nutrient uptake. Moreover, there is no simple relationship of pH to nutrient availability because of the complex combination of soil types, soil moisture regimes and meteorological factors.

Soil Organisms

Promoting the viability of beneficial soil organisms is an element of soil conservation; moreover this includes macroscopic species, notably the earthworm, as well as microorganisms. Positive effects of the earthworm are known well, as to aeration and promotion of macronutrient availability. When worms excrete egesta in the form of casts, a balanced selection of minerals and plant nutrients is made into a form accessible for root uptake. US research shows that earthworm casts are five times richer in available nitrogen, seven times richer in available phosphates and eleven times richer in available potash than the surrounding upper150 mm of soil. The weight of casts produced may be greater than 4.5 kg per worm per year. By burrowing, the earthworm is of value in creating soil porosity, creating channels enhancing the processes of aeration and drainage.

Soil microorganisms play a vital role in macronutrient wildlife. For example, nitrogen fixation is carried out by free-living or symbiotic bacteria. These bacteria have the nitrogenase enzyme that combines gaseous nitrogen with hydrogen to produce ammonia, which is then further converted by the bacteria to make other organic compounds. Some nitrogen fixing bacteria such as rhizobia live in the root nodules of legumes. Here they form a mutualistic relationship with the plant, producing ammonia in exchange for carbohydrates. In the case of the carbon cycle, carbon is transferred within the biosphere as heterotrophs feed on other organisms. This process includes the uptake of dead organic material (detritus) by fungi and bacteria in the form of fermentation or decay phenomena.

Mycorrhizae are symbiotic associations between soil-dwelling fungi and the roots of vascular plants. fungi helps increase the availability of minerals, water, and organic nutrients to the plant, while extracting sugars and amino acids from the plant. There are two main types, endomycorrhizae (which penetrate the roots) and ectomycorrhizae (which resemble 'socks', forming a sheath around the roots). They were discovered when scientists observed that certain seedlings failed to grow or prosper without soil from their native environment.

Some soil microorganisms known as extremophiles have remarkable properties of adaptation to extreme environmental conditions including temperature, pH and water deprivation.

The viability of soil organisms can be compromised when insecticides and herbicides are applied to planting regimes. Often there are unforeseen and unintended consequences of such chemical use in the form of death of impaired functioning of soil organisms. Thus any use of pesticides should only be undertaken after thorough understanding of residual toxicities upon soil organisms as well as terrestrial ecological components.

Killing soil microorganisms is a deleterious impact of slash and burn agricultural methods. With the surface temperatures generated, virtual annilation of soil and vegetative cover organisms are destroyed, and in many environments these effects can be virtually irreversible (at least for generations of mankind). Shifting cultivation is also a farming system that often employs slash and burn as one of its elements.

Systems, most of which have an adverse effect upon soil quality and plant metabolism. While the role of pH has been discussed above, heavy metals, solvents, petroleum hydrocarbons, herbicides and pesticides also contribute soil residues that are of potential concern. Some of these chemicals are totally extraneous to the agricultural landscape, but others (notably herbicides and pesticides) are intentionally introduced to serve a short term function. Many of these added chemicals have long half-lives in soil, and others degrade to produce derivative chemicals that may be either persistent or pernicious. One alternative to chemicals in agriculture is soil steaming. Steam sterilizes the soil by killing almost all beneficial and harmful micro organisms. However no harmful remains are left. Soil health may even increase since steam unlocks nutrients in the soil which may lead to better plant growth after the thermal treatment.

Typically the expense of soil contamination remediation cannot be justified in an agricultural economic analysis, since clean-up costs are generally quite high; often remediation is mandated by state and county environmental health agencies based upon human health risk issues.

Mineralization

To allow plants full realization of their phytonutrient potential, active mineralization of the soil is sometimes undertaken. This can be in the natural form of adding crushed rock or can take the form of chemical soil supplement. In either case the purpose is to combat mineral depletion of the soil. There are a broad range of minerals that can be added including common substances such as phosphorus and more exotic substances such as zinc and selenium. There is extensive research on the phase transitions of minerals in soil with aqueous contact.

The process of flooding can bring significant bedload sediment to an alluvial plain. While this effect may not be desirable if floods endanger life or if the eroded sediment originates from productive land, this process of addition to a floodplain is a natural process that can rejuvenate soil chemistry through mineralization and macronutrient addition.

12 Soil Life

Soil life or soil biota is a collective term for all the organisms living within the soil.

In a balanced soil, plants grow in an active and vibrant environment. The mineral content of the soil and its physical structure are important for their well-being, but it is the life in the earth that powers its cycles and provides its fertility. Without the activities of soil organisms, organic materials would accumulate and litter the soil surface, and there would be no food for plants. The soil biota includes:

- *Megafauna:* size range 20 mm upwards, *e.g.* moles, rabbits, and rodents.
- *Macrofauna:* size range 2-20 mm, *e.g.* woodlice, earthworms, beetles, centipedes, slugs, snails, ants, and harvestmen.
- *Mesofauna:* size range 100 micrometre-2 mm, *e.g.* tardigrades, mites and springtails.
- *Microfauna and Microflora:* size range 1-100 micrometres, *e.g.* yeasts, bacteria (commonly actinobacteria), fungi, protozoa, roundworms, and rotifers.

Of these, bacteria and fungi play key roles in maintaining a healthy soil. They act as decomposers that break down organic materials to produce detritus and other breakdown products. Soil detritivores, like earthworms, ingest detritus and decompose it. Saprotrophs, well represented by fungi and bacteria, extract soluble nutrients from delitro.

Bacteria

Bacteria are single-celled organisms, and are the most numerous denizens of agriculture, with populations ranging from 100 million to 3 billion in a gram. They are capable of very rapid reproduction by binary fission (dividing into two) in favourable conditions. One bacterium is capable of producing 16 million more in just 24 hours. Most soil bacteria live in close proximity to plant roots and are often referred to as rhizobacteria. Bacteria live in soil water, including the film of moisture surrounding soil particles, and some are able to swim by means of flagella. The majority of the beneficial soil-dwelling bacteria need oxygen (and are thus termed aerobic bacteria), whilst those that do not require air are referred to as anaerobic, and tend to cause putrefaction of dead organic matter. Aerobic bacteria are most active in a soil that is moist (but not saturated, as this will deprive aerobic bacteria of the air that they require), and neutral soil pH, and where there is plenty of food (carbohydrates and micronutrients from organic matter) available. Hostile conditions will not completely kill bacteria; rather, the bacteria will stop growing and get into a dormant stage, and those individuals with pro-adaptive mutations may compete better in the new conditions. Gram positive bacteria produce spores in order to wait for more favourable circumstances, and Gram negative bacteria gets into a 'non-culturable' stage.

From the organic gardener's point of view, the important roles that bacteria play are:

Nitrification

Nitrification is a vital part of the nitrogen cycle wherein certain bacteria (which manufacture their own carbohydrate supply without using the process of photosynthesis) are able to transform nitrogen in the form of ammonium, which is produced by the decomposition of proteins, into nitrates, which are available to growing plants, and once again converted to proteins.

Nitrogen Fixation

In another part of the cycle, the process of nitrogen fixation constantly puts additional nitrogen into biological circulation. This is carried out by free-living nitrogen-fixing bacteria in the soil or water such as *Azotobacter*, or by those that live in close symbiosis with leguminous plants, such as rhizobia. These bacteria form colonies in nodules they create on the roots of peas, beans, and related species. These are able to convert nitrogen from the atmosphere into nitrogen-containing organic substances.

Denitrification

While nitrogen fixation converts nitrogen from the atmosphere into organic compounds, a series of processes called denitrification returns an approximately equal amount of nitrogen to the atmosphere. Denitrifying bacteria tend to be anaerobes, or facultatively anaerobes (can alter between the oxygen dependent and oxygen independent types of metabolisms), including *Achromobacter* and *Pseudomonas*. The putrefaction process caused by oxygen-free conditions converts nitrates and nitrites in soil into nitrogen gas or into gaseous compounds such as nitrous oxide or nitric oxide. In excess, denitrification can lead to overall losses of available soil nitrogen and subsequent loss of soil fertility. However, fixed nitrogen may circulate many times between organisms and the soil before denitrification returns it to the atmosphere.

Actinobacteria

Actinobacteria are critical in the decomposition of organic matter and in humus formation, and their presence is responsible for the sweet 'earthy' aroma associated with a good healthy soil. They require plenty of air and a pH between 6.0 and 7.5, but are more tolerant of dry conditions than most other bacteria and fungi.

Fungi

A gram of garden soil can contain around one million fungi, such as yeasts and moulds. Fungi have no chlorophyll, and are not able to photosynthesise; besides, they can't use atmospheric carbon dioxide as a source of carbon, therefore they are chemo-heterotrophic, meaning that, like animals, they require a chemical source of energy rather than being able to use light as an energy source, as well as organic substrates to get carbon for growth and development.

Many fungi are parasitic, often causing disease to their living host plant, although some have beneficial relationships with living plants as we shall see below. In terms of soil and humus creation, the most important fungi tend to be saprotrophic, that is, they live on dead or decaying organic matter, thus breaking it down and converting it to forms that are available to the higher plants. A succession of fungi species will colonise the dead matter, beginning with those that use sugars and starches, which are succeeded by those that are able to break down cellulose and lignins.

Fungi spread underground by sending long thin threads known as mycelium throughout the soil; these threads can be observed throughout many soils and compost heaps. From the mycelia the fungi is able to throw up its fruiting bodies, the visible part above the soil (*e.g.*, mushrooms, toadstools and puffballs), which may contain millions of spores. When the fruiting body bursts, these spores are dispersed through the air to settle in fresh environments, and are able to lie dormant for up to years until the right conditions for their activation arise or the right food is made available.

Mycorrhizae

Those fungi that are able to live symbiotically with living plants, creating a relationship that is beneficial to both, are known as Mycorrhizae (from *myco* meaning fungal and *rhiza* meaning root). Plant root hairs are invaded by the mycelia of the mycorrhiza, which lives partly in the soil and partly in the root, and may either cover the length of the root hair as a sheath or be concentrated around its tip. The mycorrhiza obtains the carbohydrates that it requires from the root, in return providing the plant with nutrients including nitrogen and moisture. Later the plant roots will also absorb the mycelium into its own tissues.

Beneficial mycorrhizal associations are to be found in many of our edible and flowering crops. Shewell Cooper suggests that these include at least 80 per cent of the *brassica* and *solanum* families (including tomatoes and potatoes), as well as the majority of tree species, especially in forest and woodlands. Here the mycorrhizae create a fine underground mesh that extends greatly beyond the limits of the tree's roots, greatly increasing their feeding range and actually causing neighbouring trees to become physically interconnected. The benefits of mycorrhizal relations to their plant partners are not limited to nutrients, but can be essential for plant reproduction: in situations where little light is able to reach the forest floor, such as the North American pine forests, a young seedling cannot obtain sufficient light to photosynthesise for itself and will not grow properly in a sterile soil. But if the ground is underlain by a mycorrhizal mat then the developing seedling will throw down roots that can link with the fungal threads and through them obtain the nutrients it needs, often indirectly obtained from its parents or neighbouring trees.

David Attenborough points out the plant/fungi/animal relationship that creates a 'Three-way harmonious trio' to be found in forest ecosystems wherein the plant/fungi symbiosis is enhanced by animals such as the wild boar, deer, mice or flying squirrel, which feed upon the fungi's fruiting bodies, including truffles, and cause their further spread (*Private Life of Plants*, 1995). A greater understanding of the complex relationships that pervade natural systems is one of the major justifications of the organic gardener, in refraining from the use of artificial chemicals and the damage these might cause.

Earthworm

Earthworm is the common name for the largest members of Oligochaeta (which is either a class or subclass depending on the author) in the phylum Annelida. In classical systems they were placed in the order *Opisthopora,* on the basis of the male pores opening posterior to the female pores, even though the internal male segments are anterior to the female. Theoretical cladistic studies have placed them instead in the suborder *Lumbricina* of the order Haplotaxida, but this may again soon change. Folk names for the earthworm include 'dew-worm', 'rainworm', 'night crawler' and 'angleworm' (due to its use as fishing bait).

Earthworms are also called *megadriles* (or big worms), as opposed to the microdriles (or small worms) in the families Tubificidae, Lumbriculidae, and Enchytraeidae, among others. The megadriles are characterized by having a distinct clitellum (which is much more obvious than the single-layered one of the microdriles) and a vascular system with true capillaries.

Anatomy

The basic body plan of an earthworm is a tube, the digestive system, within a tube, the muscular slimy, moist outer body. The body is annular, formed of segments that are most specialized in the anterior. Earthworms have a simple circulatory system. They have two main blood vessels that extend through the length of their body: a ventral blood vessel which leads the blood to the posterior end, and a dorsal blood vessel which leads to the anterior end. The dorsal vessel is contractile and pumps blood forward, where it is pumped into the ventral vessel by a series of 'hearts' (aortic arches) which vary in number in the different taxa. A typical lumbricid will have 9 hearts. The blood is distributed from the ventral vessel into capillaries on the body wall and other organs and into a vascular sinus in the gut wall, where gases and nutrients are exchanged. This arrangement may be complicated in the various groups by suboesophageal, supraoesophageal, parietal and neural vessels, but the basic arrangement holds in all earthworms. Most earthworms are decomposers feeding on undecayed leaf and other plant matter, others are more geophagous.

Reproduction

Earthworms are hermaphrodites: They typically have two pairs of testes, surrounded by 2 pairs of testes sacs. There are 2 or 4 pairs of seminal vesicles which produce, store and release the sperm via the male pores, and ovaries and ovipores in segment 13 that release eggs via female pores on segment 14. However, most also have one or more pairs of spermathecae (depending on the species) that are internal sacs which receive and store sperm from the other worm in copulation. Some species use external spermatophores for transfer instead.

Copulation and reproduction are separate processes in earthworms. The mating pair overlap front ends ventrally and each exchanges sperm with the other. The clitellum becomes very reddish to pinkish in color. The cocoon, or egg case, is secreted by the clitellum band which is near the front of the worm, but behind the spermathecae. Some time after copulation, long after the worms have separated, the clitellum secretes the cocoon which forms a ring around the worm. The worm then backs out of the ring, and as it does so, injects its own eggs and the other worm's sperm into it. As the worm slips out, the ends of the cocoon seal to form a vaguely lemon-shaped incubator (cocoon) in which the embryonic worms develop. They emerge as small, but fully formed earthworms, except for a lack of the sex structures, which develop later in about 60 to 90 days. They attain full size in about one year, sometimes sooner. Scientists predict that the average lifespan under field conditions is 4–8 years, still most garden varieties live only one to two years. Several common earthworm species are mostly parthenogenetic, that is, with asexual reproduction resulting in clones.

Regeneration

Earthworms have the facility to regenerate lost segments, but this ability varies between species and depends on the extent of the damage. Stephenson (1930) devoted a chapter of his monograph to this topic, while G.E. Gates spent 20 years studying regeneration in a variety of species, but 'because little interest was shown', Gates (1972) only published a few of his findings that, nevertheless, show it is theoretically possible to grow two whole worms from a bisected specimen in certain species. Gates's reports included:

- *Eisenia fetida* (Savigny, 1826) with head regeneration, in an anterior direction, possible at each intersegmental level back to and including 23/24, while tails were regenerated at any levels behind 20/21.
- *Lumbricus terrestris* Linneus, 1758 replacing anterior segments from as far back as 13/14 and 16/17 but tail regeneration was never found.
- *Perionyx excavatus* Perrier, 1872 readily regenerated lost parts of the body, in an anterior direction from as far back as 17/18, and in a posterior direction as far forward as 20/21.
- *Lampito mauritii* Kinberg, 1867 with regeneration in anterior direction at all levels back to 25/26 and tail regeneration from 30/31; head regeneration was sometimes believed to be caused by internal amputation resulting from *Sarcophaga* sp. larval infestation.
- *Criodrilus lacuum* Hoffmeister, 1845 also has prodigious regenerative capacity with 'head' regeneration from as far back as 40/41.

Earthworms can be seen on the surface after heavy rain storms flood the soil because, despite needing a moist environment to allow the diffusion of gases across their skin membrane, the soil becomes saturated and they begin to drown. Earthworms also come to the surface during rain to mate. To protect themselves they escape to the surface, but if the ground is unnaturally hard they may later become stranded and die from exposure. This is why they are seen in places like driveways after a storm. However, certain earthworm species can survive immersion for several days in oxygenated water.

An alternative hypothesis concerning this behaviour is that as some species (notably *Lumbricus terrestris*) come to the surface to mate they may become stranded. However, as this behaviour is limited to only a few species and *L. terrestris* is rarely, if ever, one of those found stranded on impermeable surfaces, this hypothesis does not seem a very likely explanation.

Another hypothesis is that the worms may be using the moist conditions on the surface to travel more quickly than they can underground, thus colonizing new areas more quickly. Since the relative humidity is higher during and after rain, they do not become dehydrated. This is a dangerous activity in the daytime, since earthworms die quickly when exposed to direct sunlight with its strong UV content, and are more vulnerable to predators such as birds.

A further hypothesis is that, as there are many other organisms in the ground as well, and their respiration increases carbon dioxide, this gas may dissolve into the rainwater to form carbonic acid. As the soil becomes too acidic for the worms, they seek a more neutral environment on the soil.

Locomotion and Importance to Soil

Earthworms travel underground by the means of waves of muscular contractions which alternately shorten and lengthen the body. The shortened part is anchored to the surrounding soil by tiny claw-like bristles (setae) set along its segmented length. (In all the body segments except the first, last and clitellum, there is a ring of S-shaped setae, embedded in the epidermal pit of each segment, perichaetine) The whole burrowing process is aided by the secretion of lubricating mucus. Worms can make gurgling noises underground when disturbed as a result of the worm moving through its lubricated tunnels. They also work as biological 'pistons' forcing air through the tunnels as they move. Thus earthworm activity aerates and mixes the soil, and is constructive to mineralization and nutrient uptake by vegetation. Certain species of earthworm come to the surface and graze on the higher concentrations of organic matter present there, mixing it with the mineral soil. Because a high level of organic matter mixing is associated with soil fertility, an abundance of earthworms is beneficial to the organic gardener. In fact as long ago as 1881 Charles Darwin wrote:

> It may be doubted whether there are many other animals which have played so important a part in the history of the world, as have these lowly organized creatures.

Benefits

The major benefits of earthworm activities to soil fertility can be summarized as:

- **Biological**: In many soils, earthworms play a major role in converting large pieces of organic matter (*e.g.* dead leaves) into rich humus, and thus improving soil fertility. This is achieved by the worm's actions of pulling down below any organic matter deposited on the dried dirt, such as leaf fall or manure, either for food or when it needs to plug its burrow. Once in the burrow, the worm will shred the leaf and partially digest it, then mingle it with the earth by saturating it with intestinal secretions. Worm casts can contain 40 per cent more humus than the top 9″ of soil in which the worm is living.

- **Chemical**: As well as dead organic matter, the earthworm also ingests any other soil particles that are small enough — including stones up to $^1/_{20}$ of an inch (1.25 mm) across — into its gizzard wherein minute fragments of grit grind everything into a fine paste which is then digested in the intestine. When the worm excretes this in the form of casts which are deposited on the surface or deeper in the soil, minerals and plant nutrients are made available in an accessible form. Investigations in the US show that fresh earthworm casts are 5 times richer in available nitrogen, 7 times richer in available phosphates and 11 times richer in available potash than the surrounding upper 6 inches (150 mm) of soil. In conditions where there is plenty of available humus, the weight of casts produced may be greater than 4.5 kg (10 lb) per worm per year, in itself an indicator of why it pays the gardener or farmer to keep worm populations high.
- **Physical**: By its burrowing actions, the earthworm is of great value in keeping the soil structure open, creating a multitude of channels which allow the processes of both aeration and drainage to occur. Permaculture co-founder Bill Mollison points out that by sliding in their tunnels, earthworms "act as an innumerable army of pistons pumping air in and out of the soils on a 24 hour cycle (more rapidly at night)" . Thus the earthworm not only creates passages for air and water to traverse, but is itself a vital component in the living biosystem that is healthy soil. Earthworms continue to move through the soil due to the excretion of mucus into the soil that acts as a lubricant for easier movement of the worm.

The earthworm's existence cannot be taken for granted. Dr. W.E. Shewell Cooper observed "tremendous numerical differences between adjacent gardens" (*Soil, Humus and Health*), and worm populations are affected by a host of environmental factors, many of which can be influenced by good management practices on the part of the gardener or farmer.

Darwin estimated that arable land contains up to 53,000 worms per acre ($13/m^2$), but more recent research from Rothamsted Experimental Station has produced figures suggesting that even poor soil may support 250,000/acre ($62/m^2$), whilst rich fertile farmland may have up to 1,750,000/acre ($432/m^2$), meaning that the weight of earthworms beneath the farmer's soil could be greater than that of his livestock upon its surface. One thing is certain however: rich, fertile soil that is cared for organically and well-fed and husbanded by its steward will reap its reward in a healthy worm population, whilst denuded, overworked, and eroded land will almost certainly contain fewer, scrawny, undernourished specimens.

Earthworms as Invasive Species

From a total of around 6,000 species, only about 120 species are widely distributed around the world. These are the peregrine or cosmopolitan earthworms.

North America

A total of approximately 182 earthworm taxa in 12 families are reported from America north of Mexico, *i.e.*, USA and Canada, of which 60 (ca. 33%) are exotic/introduced. Only two genera of Lumbricid earthworms are indigenous to North America while introduced genera have spread to areas where earthworms did not formerly exist, especially in the north where forest development relies on a large amount of undecayed leaf matter. When worms decompose that leaf layer, the ecology may shift making the habitat unsurvivable for certain species of trees, ferns and wildflowers. Another possible ecologic impact of greater earthworm numbers: larger earthworms (*e.g.* the night crawler, *Lumbricus terrestris*, and the Alabama jumper, *Amynthas agrestis*) can be eaten by adult salamanders, and when the salamanders do consume the earthworms they are more successful at reproduction. However, those earthworms are too large for juvenile salamanders to consume, which leads to a net loss in salamander population.

Currently there is no economically feasible method for controlling invasive earthworms in forests. Earthworms normally spread slowly, but can be quickly introduced by human activities such as construction earthmoving, or by fishermen releasing bait, or by plantings from other areas.

Australia

Australia has 650 known species of native earthworm that survive in both rich and in nutrient-poor conditions where they may be sensitive to changes in the environment. Introduced species are commonly found in agricultural environments along with persistent natives. Most of the 75 or so exotics have been accidentally introduced into Australia. The total species numbers are predicted to exceed 2,000.

Special Habitats

While, as the name *earthworm* suggests, the main habitat of earthworms is in soil, the situation is more complicated than that. The brandling worm *Eisenia fetida* lives in decaying plant matter and manure. *Arctiostrotus vancouverensis* from Vancouver Island and the Olympic Peninsula is generally found in decaying conifer logs or in extremely acidic humus. *Aporrectodea limicola* and *Sparganophilus* and several others are found in mud in streams. Some species are arboreal. Even in the soil species, there are special habitats, such as soils derived from serpentine which have an earthworm fauna of their own.

Ecology

Earthworms are classified into three main eco-physiological categories:

1. leaf litter/compost dwelling worms (epigeic) *e.g. Eisenia fetida*;
2. topsoil or subsoil dwelling worms (endogeics); and
3. worms that construct permanent deep burrows through which they visit the surface to obtain plant material for food, such as leaves (anecic), *e.g. Lumbricus terrestris*.

Earthworm populations depend on both physical and chemical properties of the soil, such as soil temperature, moisture, pH, salts, aeration and texture, as well as available food, and the ability of the species to reproduce and disperse. One of the most important environmental factors is pH, but earthworms vary in their preferences. Most earthworms favour neutral to slightly acidic soil. However, *Lumbricus terrestris* are still present in a pH of 5.4 and *Dendrobaena octaedra* at a pH of 4.3 and some Megascolecidae are present in extremely acid humic soils. Soil pH may also influence the numbers of worms that go into diapause. The more acid the soil, the sooner worms go into diapause, and remain in diapause the longest time at a pH of 6.4.

Earthworms form the base of many food chains. They are preyed upon by many species of birds (*e.g.* starlings, thrushes, gulls, crows, European Robins and American Robins), snakes, mammals (*e.g.* bears, foxes, hedgehogs, moles) and invertebrates (*e.g.* ground beetles and other beetles, snails, slugs). Earthworms have many internal parasites including Protozoa, Platyhelminthes, Nematodes; they can found in the worms' blood, seminal vesicles, coelom, intestine, or in the cocoons.The application of chemical fertilizers, sprays and dusts can have a disastrous effect on earthworm populations. Nitrogenous fertilizers tend to create acid conditions, which are fatal to the worms, and often dead specimens are to be found on the surface following the application of substances like DDT, lime sulphur and lead arsenate. In Australia, the use of superphosphate on pastures almost completely wiped out the giant Gippsland earthworm.

Therefore, the most reliable way to maintain or increase the levels of worm population in the soil is to avoid the application of artificial chemicals. Adding organic matter, preferably as a surface mulch, on a regular basis will provide them with their food and nutrient requirements, and also creates the optimum conditions of heat (cooler in summer and warmer in winter) and moisture to stimulate their activity.

A recent threat to earthworm populations in the UK is the New Zealand Flatworm (*Artiposthia triangulata*), which feeds upon the earthworm, but in the UK has no natural predator itself. At present sightings of the New Zealand flatworm have been mainly localised, but this is no reason for complacency as it has spread extensively since its introduction in 1960 through contaminated soil and plant pots. Any sightings of the flatworm should be reported to the Scottish Crop Research Institute, which is monitoring its spread.

Economic Impact

Various species of worms are used in vermiculture, the practice of feeding organic waste to earthworms to decompose (digest) it, a form of composting by the use of worms. These are usually *Eisenia fetida* (or its close relative *Eisenia andrei*) or the Brandling worm, also known as the Tiger worm or Red Wiggler, and are distinct from soil-dwelling earthworms.

Earthworms are sold all over the world. The earthworm market is sizable. According to Doug Collicut, "In 1980, 370 million worms were exported from Canada, with a Canadian export value of $13 million and an American retail value of $54 million."

Earthworms are also sold as food for human consumption. Noke is a culinary term used by the Maori of New Zealand to refer to earthworms which are considered delicacies.

A report on biodiversity published by the Irish Government in May 2008 estimated the activities of the earthworm to be worth a minimum of C723 millon per annum to Irish agriculture.

Taxonomy and Distribution

The families, with distribution of the main ones:

- Alluroididae
- *Eudrilidae:* Tropical Africa
- *Glossoscolecidae:* Central and northern South America
- *Lumbricidae:* Temperate Northern Hemisphere from Vancouver Island, Canada to Japan, mostly Eurasia
- *Hormogastridae:* Europe
- Ailoscolidae
- Lutodrilidae
- *Sparganophilidae:* North America
- Criodrilidae
- Almidae Africa, South America
- *Ocnerodrilidae:* Central and South America, Africa
- Acanthodrilidae: Africa, midland and southeastern North America, Central and South America, Australia and Oceania. Octochaetidae: Central/South America, western Africa, India, New Zealand, Australia. Exxidae: Central America/Caribbean. Megascolecidae: South East Asia, Australasia and Oceania, northwestern North America. Microchaetidae.

13 Soil pH

Soil pH is a measure of the soil acidity or soil alkalinity. An acid solution has a pH value less than 7. While a basic solution always has a pH larger than 7, an alkaline solution (*i.e.*, a solution with positive acid neutralizing capacity), can also be defined as the negative logarithm of hydrogen ions in the soil. It therefore does not necessarily have a pH larger than 7. For details on the relation between pH and ANC, see acid neutralizing capacity.

Importance

Soil pH is an important consideration for farmers and gardeners for several reasons:

- Many plants and soil life forms have a preference for either alkaline or acidic conditions, affecting the choice of crop or plant that can be grown without intervention to adjust the pH.
- Diseases affecting plants also tend to thrive in soil with a particular pH range.
- The pH can affect the availability of nutrients in the soil.

Nutrient Availability in Relation to Soil pH

The majority of food crops prefer a neutral or slightly acidic soil (pH 7). Some plants, however, prefer more acidic (*e.g.*, potatoes, strawberries) or alkaline (*e.g.*, brassicas) conditions.

Once the cation exchange surface has become depleted of these ions, however, the concentration in soil solution can be quite low and is largely determined by the weathering rate. The weathering rate in turn is dependent on such things as mineralogy (*e.g.*, presence of easily weathered minerals), surface area (*i.e.*, the soil texture), soil moisture (*i.e.*, how large a fraction of the mineral surface area that is wet), pH, concentration of base cations such as Ca, Mg and K as well as concentration of aluminium. The amount of plant available nutrients is a much more difficult issue than soil solution concentrations.

It is thus important to realize that there exists no simple relation between soil solution concentration of Ca, Mg and K and reasonable pH-values. The reason for this is that Ca, Mg and K are base cations, *i.e.*, cations of strong bases, and strong bases are fully dissociated at the pH-ranges occurring in most natural waters. However, as the soil solution pH is dependent on mineral weathering, and mineral weathering increases pH by releasing Ca, Mg and K, a soil which is rich in easily weatherable minerals tends to have both a higher pH and higher soil solution concentration of Ca, Mg and K. On the other hand deposition of sulphate, nitrate and to some extent ammonia decrease the pH of soil solution essentially without affecting Ca, Mg and K concentrations whereas deposition of sea salt increases Ca, Mg and K concentrations without having much of an effect on soil solution pH.

When interpreting soil solution pH values it is essential to take into account the method by which pH has been measured. Depending on whether or not the water has been equilibrated with ambient CO_2 pressure or not the pH reported from the same site may be either high or low. This is simply because the carbon dioxide pressure deep down in the soil might be 10-20 times higher than the ambient pressure due to decomposition of organic material. The higher carbon dioxide pressure result in more carbonic acid and hence a lower pH. Furthermore, soil solution can be extracted from the soil in many ways, for example by lysimeters, zero-tension lysimeters, centrifugation, extraction with $CaCl_2$, overhead shaking of soil sample with added water.

The $CaCl_2$ extraction method does not give the actual soil solution pH but rather a mix between soil solution pH and what is easily available, for example through cation exchange. Also when mixing soil samples with water and using overhead shakers (or similar) the result is a mix between actual soil solution and cation exchange, although the hope is that the extracted water will be similar to the actual soil solution in most respects. If centrifugation or pressurised lysimeters are used, care must be taken that the extracted water does not include water that is not readily available (think wilting point and crystal water). Naturally, taking a sample introduces a disturbance of the system, which can for example result in a change in nutrient uptake and decomposition rates (*e.g.*, due to cutting of fine roots when placing the lysimeter).

Many nutrient cations such as zinc (Zn^{2+}), aluminium (Al^{3+}), iron (Fe^{2+}), copper (Cu^{2+}), cobalt (Co^{2+}), and manganese (Mn^{2+}) are soluble and available for uptake by plants below pH 5.0, although their availability can be excessive and thus toxic in more acidic conditions. In more alkaline conditions they are less available, and symptoms of nutrient deficiency may result, including thin plant stems, yellowing (chlorosis) or mottling of leaves, and slow or stunted growth.

pH levels also affect the complex interactions among soil chemicals. Phosphorus (P) for example requires a pH between 6.0 and 7.5 and becomes chemically immobile outside this range, forming insoluble compounds with iron (Fe) and aluminium (Al) in acid soils and with calcium (Ca) in calcareous soils.

How Acidic Soil Forms

Rainfall filters through trees and into the ground, where it dissolves limestone sediment and other alkaline minerals that help neutralize soil acidity. The woodland floor is carpeted in needles of conifers, leaves of hardwood trees, and other dead plant matter, most of which increase soil acidity as they decompose. Unless this woodland is on top of a huge deposit of alkaline material such as limestone or serpentine, the soil will tend to be acidic.

Soils and Acidity

Under conditions in which rainfall exceeds evapotranspiration (leaching) during most of the year, the basic soil cations (Ca, Mg, K) are gradually depleted and replaced with cations held in colloidal soil reserves, leading to soil acidity. Clay soils often contain iron and aluminium hydroxides, which affect the retention and availability of fertilizer cations and anions in acidic soils.

Soil acidification may also occur by addition of hydrogen, due to decomposition of organic matter, acid-forming fertilizers, and exchange of basic cations for H^+ by the roots. Soil acidity is reduced by volatilization and denitrification of nitrogen. Under flooded conditions, the soil pH value increases.

In addition, the following nitrate fertilizers — calcium nitrate, magnesium nitrate, potassium nitrate and sodium nitrate — also increase the soil pH value. Some alkaline soils have calcium in the form of limestone that is not chemically available to plants.

Factors Affecting Soil pH

The pH value of a soil is influenced by the kinds of parent materials from which the soil was formed. Soils developed from basic rocks generally have higher pH values than those formed from acid rocks.

Rainfall also affects soil pH. Water passing through the soil leaches basic nutrients such as calcium and magnesium from the soil. They are replaced by acidic elements such as aluminium and iron. For this reason, soils formed under high rainfall conditions are more acidic than those formed under arid (dry) conditions.

Soil Life and pH

A pH level of around 6.3-6.8 is also the optimum range preferred by most soil bacteria, although fungi, moulds, and anaerobic bacteria have a broader tolerance and tend to multiply at lower pH values. Therefore, more acidic soils tend to be susceptible to souring and putrefaction, rather than undergoing the sweet decay processes associated with the decay of organic matter, which immeasurably benefit the soil. These processes also prefer near-neutral conditions.

pH and Plant Diseases

Many plant diseases are caused or exacerbated by extremes of pH, sometimes because this makes essential nutrients unavailable to crops or because the soil itself is unhealthy. For example, chlorosis of leaf vegetables and potato scab occur in overly alkaline conditions, and acidic soils can cause clubroot in brassicas.

Determining pH

A map of the pH level is a mosaic, varying according to soil crumb structure, on the surface of colloids, and at microsites. The pH also exhibits vertical gradients, tending to be more acidic in surface mulches and alkaline where evaporation, wormcasts, and capillary action draw bases up to the soil surface. It also varies on a macro level depending on factors such as slope, rocks, and vegetation type. Therefore the pH should be measured regularly and at various points within the land in question. Methods of determining pH include:

- *Observation of soil profile*. Strongly acidic soils often have poor incorporation of the organic surface layer with the underlying mineral layer. The mineral horizons are distinctively layered in many cases, with a pale eluvial (E) horizon beneath the organic surface; this E is underlain by a darker B horizon in a classic podzol horizon sequence. This is a very rough gauge of acidity as there is no correlation between thickness of the E and soil pH. E horizons a few feet thick in Florida usually have pH just above 5 (merely 'strongly acid') while E horizons a few inches thick in New England are 'extremely acid' with pH readings of 4.5 or below. In the southern Blue Ridge Mountains there are 'ultra acid' soils, pH below 3.5, which have no E horizon.
- *Observation of predominant flora*. Calcifuge plants (those that prefer an acidic soil) include *Erica, Rhododendron* and nearly all other Ericaceae species, many *Betula* birch), *Digitalis* foxgloves), gorse, and Scots Pine. Calcicole (lime loving) plants include *Fraxinus* Ash), Honeysuckle (*Lonicera*), Buddleia, *Cornus* spp (dogwoods), Lilac(*Syringa*) and *Clematis* spp.
- *Observation of symptoms* that might indicate acidic or alkaline conditions, such as occurrence of the plant diseases mentioned above or salinisation of alkaline soils. The house hydrangea (*Hydrangea macrophylla*) produces pink flowers at pH values of 6.8 or higher, and blue flowers at pH 6.0 or below:
    - *Use of an inexpensive pH testing kit* based on barium sulphate in powdered form, where in a small sample of soil is mixed with water which changes colour according to the acidity/alkalinity.
    - *Use of litmus paper*. A small sample of soil is mixed with distilled water, into which a strip of litmus paper is inserted. If the soil is acidic the paper turns red, if alkaline, blue.

- *Use of a commercially available electronic pH metre*, in which a rod is inserted into moistened soil and measures the concentration of hydrogen ions.

Increasing Soil pH

The aim when attempting to adjust soil acidity is not so much to neutralise the pH as to replace lost cation nutrients, particularly calcium. This can be achieved by adding limestone to the soil, which is available in various forms.

Agricultural lime (ground limestone or chalk) is used for soil liming. These natural forms of calcium carbonate are probably the cheapest form of lime for gardening and agricultural use and can be applied at any time of the year. These forms are slow reacting, thus their effect on soil fertility and plant growth is steady and long lasting. Ground lime should be applied to clay and heavy soils at a rate of about 500 to 1,000 g/m^2 (1 to 2 lb/yd^2 or 4,500 to 9,000 lb/ac). The concept of "corrected lime potential" to define the degree of base saturation in soils became the basis for procedures now used in soil testing laboratories to determine the "lime requirement" of soils.

Quicklime and Slaked Lime

The former is produced by burning rock limestone in kilns. It is highly caustic and cannot be applied directly to the soil. Quicklime reacts with water to produce slaked, or hydrated, lime, thus quicklime is spread around agricultural land in heaps to absorb rain and atmospheric moisture and form slaked lime, which is then spread on the soil. Quicklime should be applied to heavy clays at a rate of about 400 to 500 g/m^2 (0.75 to 1 lb/yd^2 or 3,600 to 4,500 lb/ac), hydrated lime at 250 to 500 g/m^2 (0.5 to 1 lb/yd^2). However, quicklime and hydrated lime are very fast acting and are not suitable for inclusion in an organic system. Their use is prohibited under the standards of both The Soil Association and the Henry Doubleday Research Association.

Calcium sulphate (gypsum) cannot be used to amend soil acidity. It is a common myth that gypsum affects soil acidity However, gypsum does reduce aluminium toxicity. Because gypsum is more soluble than alkaline earth carbonates, it is recommended for the treatment of acidic subsoils.

Reducing soil pH

- The pH of an alkaline soil is lowered by adding sulfur, iron sulphates or aluminium sulphate, although these tend to be expensive, and the effects short term.
- Urea, urea phosphate, ammonium nitrate, ammonium phosphates, ammonium sulphate and monopotassium phosphate also lower soil pH.
- Fertilizers often also affect a slightly more acidic soil since this increases uptake of nutrients.
- Decayed vegetable matter, compost, stable manure, urea, etc.

Examples of Plant Preferences

Acid soil of pH 4.5-5.0 Some plants will not tolerate higher pH such as Blueberry, Bilberry, Heather, Cranberry, Orchid, Azalea, for blue Hydrangea (less acidic for pink) , Sweet Gum, Pin Oak.

Acid soil of pH 5.0 - 5.5 Plants for acid soil in this range include Parsley, Potato, Tomato, Heather, Conifers, Pine, Sweet Potato, Maize, Millet, Oars, Tye, Radish, Ferns, Iris, Orchids, Rhododendron, Camellia, Daphne and Boronia.

Acid soil of pH 5.5 - 6.0 Plants for a moderately acid soil include Bean, Brussels Sprouts, Carrot, Choko, Endive, Kohl Rabi, Peanuts, Rhubarb, Soyabean, Crimson Clover, Aster, Begonia, Canna, Daffodil, Jonquil, Larkspur, Petunia, Primrose, Violet and most bulbs.

Acid soil of pH 6.0 - 6.5 Plants that prefer this soil include Broccoli, Cabbage, Cauliflower, Cucumber, Egg Plant,

Pea, Sweet Corn, Pumpkin, Squash, Turnip, Red Clover, Sweet Clover, White Clover, Candytuft, Gladiolus, Iceland Poppy, Pansy, Rose, Snapdragon, Viola, Wallflower, Zinnea and Strawberry.

Acid soil of pH 6.5 - 7.0 Plants that favor very mildly acid soil are Asparagus, Beet, Celery, Lettuce, Melons, Onion, Parsnip, Spinach, Lucerne, Carnation, Chrysanthemum, Dahlia, Stock, Sweet Pea and Tulip.

14 Alkali Soils

Alkali, or alkaline soils are clay soils with high pH (> 9), a poor soil structure and a low infiltration capacity. Often they have a hard calcareous layer at 0.5 to 1 metre. depth (in India this layer is called 'kankar'). Alkali soils owe their unfavourable physico-chemical properties mainly to the dominating presence of sodium carbonate which causes the soil to *swell*. They derive their name from the alkali metal group of elements to which the sodium belongs and that can induce basicity. Sometimes these soils are also referred to as *(alkaline) sodic soils*.

Causes

The causes of soil alkalinity are natural or they can be man-made.

The natural cause is the presence of soil minerals producing sodium carbonate (Na_2CO_3) upon weathering.

The man-made cause is the application of irrigation water (surface or ground water) containing a relatively high proportion of sodium bicarbonates.

Occurrence

The extent of alkaline soils is not precisely known.

Agricultural Problems

Alkaline soils are difficult to take into agricultural production. Due to the low infiltration capacity, rain water stagnates on the soil easily and, in dry periods, irrigation is hardly possible. Agriculture is limited to crops tolerant to surface waterlogging (e.g. rice, grasses) and the productivity is low.

Chemistry

Soil alkalinity is associated with the presence of sodium carbonates or (soda) (Na_2CO_3) in the soil, either as a result of natural weathering of the soil particles or brought in by irrigation and/or flood water.

The sodium carbonate, when dissolved in water, dissociates into $2Na^+$ (two sodium cations, i.e. ions with a positive electric charge) and $CO3^=$ (a carbonate anion, i.e. an ion with a double negative electric charge).

The sodium-carbonate can react with water to produce carbon dioxide (CO_2), escaping as a gas, and sodium hydroxide (Na^+OH^-), which is alkaline (or rather basic) and gives high pH values (pH>9).

Water (H_2O) is partly dissociated into H^+ (hydrogen) and OH^- (hydroxyl) ions. The ion H^+ has a positive electric charge (+) and the hydroxyl group OH^- has a negative charge (–). In pure, neutral water, the concentration of H^+ and OH^- ions equals 10^{-7} eq/l each (respectively 10^{-7} g/l and $17x10^{-7}$ g/l), a very small concentration.

Note: 1 eq = 1 equivalent weight corresponds to as many grams of the substance as its molecular weight. It is also known as *gram-molecule* or mole. For hydrogen the hydrogen ion (H^+) the molecular weight equals 1, and for the hydroxyl group (OH^-) it equals 17. Substances with the same equivalent weight have the same positive or negative electric charge.

The pH, being the negative log value of the H^+ concentration in eq/l, is 7. Similarly, the pOH is also 7. Each unit decrease in pH indicates a tenfold increase of the H^+ concentration. Similarly, each unit increase in pH indicates a tenfold increase of the OH^- concentration.In water with dissolved salts, the concentrations of the H^+ and OH^- ions may change, but the sum of pH and pOH remains equal to 7 + 7 = 14.

Water with excess H^+ ions is called acid (pH < 6), and water with excess OH^- ions is called alkaline or rather basic (pH > 8). Soil moisture with pH < 4 is called very acid and with pH > 10 very alkaline (basic).

The reaction between Na_2CO_3 and H^+O can represented as follows:

- $2Na^+ + CO3^{--} + 2H^+ + 2OH^- \rightarrow 2Na^+ + 2OH^- + H_2CO_3$

The acid H_2CO_3 is unstable and produces H_2O (water) and CO_2 (carbon dioxide gas, escaping into the atmosphere). This explains the remaining alkalinity (or rather basicity) in the form of soluble sodium hydroxide and the high pH or low pOH.

Not all sodium carbonate follows the above chemical reaction. The remaining sodium carbonate, and hence the presence of $CO_3^=$ ions, causes $CaCO_3$ (which is only slightly soluble) to precipitate as solid calcium carbonate (limestone). Hence, the calcium ions Ca^{++} are immobilized:

- $2Na^+ + CO_3^= + Ca^{++} \rightarrow 2Na+ + CaCO_3$ (solid)

Sodium exchange process between clay particles and the soil moisture.

The presence of abundant Na^+ ions in the soil solution and the precipitation of Ca^{++} ions as a solid mineral causes the clay particles, which have negative electric charges along their surfaces, to adsorb more Na^+ in the *diffuse adsorption zone* (DAZ), officially called *diffuse double layer* and, in exchange, release Ca^{++}, by which their *exchangeable sodium percentage* (ESP) is increased.

Na^+ is more mobile and has a smaller electric charge than Ca^{++} so that the thickness of the DAZ increases as more sodium is present. The thickness is also influenced by the total concentration of ions in the soil moisture in the sense that higher concentrations cause the DAZ zone to shrink.

Clay particles with considerable ESP (> 16), in contact with non-saline soil moisture have an expanded DAZ zone and the soil swells (dispersion). The phenomenon results in deterioration of the soil structure, and especially crust formation and compaction of the top layer. Hence the infiltration capacity of the soil and the water availability in the soil is reduced, whereas the surface-water-logging or runoff is increased. Seedling emergence and crop production are badly affected.

Note: Under saline conditions, the many ions in the soil solution counteract the swelling of the soil, so that saline soils usually do not have unfavorable physical properties. Alkaline soils, in principle, are not not saline since the alkalinity problem is worse as the salinity is less.

Alkalinity problems are more pronounced in clay soils than in loamy, silty or sandy soils. The clay soils containing montmorillonite or smectite (swelling clays) are more subject to alkalinity problems than illite or kaolinite clay soils. The reason is that the former types of clay have larger specific surface areas (i.e. the surface area of the soil particles divided by their volume) and higher cation exchange capacity (CEC).

Note: Certain clay minerals with almost 100 per cent ESP (i.e. almost fully sodium saturated) are called bentonite, which is used in civil engineering to place impermeable curtains in the soil, *e.g.* below dams, to prevent seepage of water.

Solutions

Alkaline soils with solid $CaCO_3$ can be reclaimed with grass cultures, ensuring the incorporation of much acidifying organic material into the soil, and leaching of the excess sodium. Deep plowing and incorporating the calcareous subsoil into the top soil also helps.

It is also possible to reclaim alkaline soils by adding acidifying minerals like pyrite.

Alternatively, gypsum (calcium sulfate, $CaSO_4 . 2H_2O$) can also be applied as a source of Ca^{++} ions to replace the sodium at the exchange complex. There must be enough natural drainage to the underground, or else an artificial subsurface drainage system must be present, to permit leaching of the excess sodium by percolation of rain and/or irrigation water through the soil profile.

To reclaim the soils completely one needs prohibitively high doses of amendments. Most efforts are therefore directed to improving the top layer only (say the first 10 cm of the soils), as the top layer is most sensitive to deterioration of the soil structure. The treatments, however, need to be repeated in a few (say 5) years time.

It will be important to refrain from irrigation with poor quality water.

The quality of the irrigation water in relation to the alkalinity hazard is expressed by the following two indexes:

1. The *sodium adsorption ratio* (SAR)

   The formula for calculating sodium adsorption ratio is:

$$SAR = \frac{[Na^+]}{v[Ca^{++}/2 + Mg^{++}/2]} = \frac{\{Na^+/23\}}{v\{Ca^{++}/40 + Mg^{++}/24\}}$$

   where: [ ] stands for concentration in milliequivalents/liter (briefly meq/l), and { } stands for concentration in mg/l.

   It is seen that Mg (Magnesium) is thought to play a similar role as Ca (Calcium).

   The SAR should not be much higher than 20 and preferably less than 10.

   When the soil has been exposed to water with a certain SAR value for some time, the ESP value tends to become about equal to the SAR value.

2. The *residual sodium carbonate* (RSC, meq/l:

   The formula for calculating residual sodium carbonate is:

   RSC = $[HCO_3^- + CO_3^=] - [Ca^{++} + Mg^{++}]$

   $= \{HCO_3^-/61 + CO_3^=/30\} - \{Ca^{++}/20 + Mg^{++}/12\}$

   which must not be much higher than 1 and preferably less than 0.5.

The above expression recognizes the presence of bicarbonates (HCO_3^-), the form in which most carbonates are dissolved.

Leaching Saline Sodic Soils

Saline soils are mostly also sodic (the predominant salt is sodium chloride), but they do not have a very high pH nor a poor infiltration rate. Upon leaching they are usually not converted into a (sodic) alkali soil as the Na^+ ions are easily removed. Therefore, saline (sodic) soils mostly do not need gypsum applications for their reclamation.

15 Limestone

Limestone is a sedimentary rock composed largely of the mineral calcite (calcium carbonate: $CaCO_3$). Like most other sedimentary rocks, limestones are comprised of grains, however, around 80-90 per cent of limestone grains are skeletal fragments of marine organisms such as coral or foraminifera. Other carbonate grains comprising limestones are ooids, peloids, intraclasts, and extraclasts. Some limestones do not consist of grains at all and are formed completly by the chemical precipitation of calcite or aragonite. *i.e.* travertine.

The solubility of limestone in water and weak acid solutions leads to karst landscapes. Regions overlying limestone bedrock tend to have fewer visible groundwater sources (ponds and streams), as surface water easily drains downward through joints in the limestone. While draining, water and organic acid from the soil slowly (over thousands or millions of years) enlarges these cracks; dissolving the calcium-carbonate and carrying it away in solution. Most cave systems are through limestone bedrock.

Description

Limestone often contains variable amounts of silica in the form of chert (aka chalcedony, flint, jasper, etc.) or siliceous skeletal fragment (sponge spicules, diatoms, radiolarins), as well as varying amounts of clay, silt and sand sized terrestrial detritus carried in by rivers. The primary source of the calcite in limestone is most commonly marine organisms. These organisms secrete shells made of aragonite or calcite and leave these shells behind after the organism dies. Some of these organisms can contruct mounds of rock known as reefs, building upon past generations. Below about 3,000 meters, water pressure and temperature causes the dissolution of calcite to increase non-linearly so that limestone typically does not form in deeper waters. Secondary calcite may also be deposited by supersaturated meteoric waters (groundwater that precipitates the material in caves). This produces speleothems such as stalagmites and stalactites. Another form taken by calcite is that of oolites (oolitic limestone) which can be recognized by its granular appearance.

Limestone makes up about 10 per cent of the total volume of all sedimentary rocks. Limestones may also form in both lacustrine and evaporite depositional environments.

Calcite can be either dissolved by groundwater or precipitated by groundwater, depending on several factors including the water temperature, pH, and dissolved ion concentrations. Calcite exhibits an unusual characteristic called retrograde solubility in which it becomes less soluble in water as the temperature increases.

When conditions are right for precipitation, calcite forms mineral coatings that cement the existing rock grains together or it can fill fractures.

Karst topography and caves develop in carbonate rocks due to their solubility in dilute acidic groundwater. Cooling groundwater or mixing of different groundwaters will also create conditions suitable for cave formation.

Coastal limestones are often eroded by organisms which bore into the rock by various means. This process is known as bioerosion. It is most common in the tropics, and it is known throughout the fossil record.

Because of impurities, such as clay, sand, organic remains, iron oxide and other materials, many limestones exhibit different colours, especially on weathered surfaces. Limestone may be crystalline, clastic, granular, or massive, depending on the method of formation. Crystals of calcite, quartz, dolomite or barite may line small cavities in the rock. Folk and Dunham classifications are used to describe limestones more precisely.

Travertine is a banded, compact variety of limestone formed along streams, particularly where there are waterfalls and around hot or cold springs. Calcium carbonate is deposited where evaporation of the water leaves a solution that is supersaturated with chemical constituents of calcite. Tufa, a porous or cellular variety of travertine, is found near waterfalls. Coquina is a poorly consolidated limestone composed of pieces of coral or shells.

During regional metamorphism that occurs during the mountain building process (orogeny) limestone recrystallizes into marble.

Limestone is a parent material of Mollisol soil group.

Limestone Landscape

Limestone is partially soluble, especially in acid, and therefore forms many erosional landforms. These include limestone pavements, pot holes, cenotes, caves and gorges. Such erosion landscapes are known as karsts. Limestone is less resistant than most igneous rocks, but more resistant than most other sedimentary rocks. Limestone is therefore usually associated with hills and downland and occurs in regions with other sedimentary rocks, typically clays.

Bands of limestone emerge from the Earth's surface in often spectacular rocky outcrops and islands. Examples include the Burren in Co. Clare, Ireland; the Verdon Gorge in France; Malham Cove in North Yorkshire and the Isle of Wight, England; on Fårö near the Swedish island of Gotland, the Niagara Escarpment in Canada/United States, Notch Peak in Utah, the Ha Long Bay National Park in Vietnam and the hills around the Lijiang River and Guilin city in China.

The Florida Keys, islands off the south coast of Florida, are composed mainly of oolitic limestone (the Lower Keys) and the carbonate skeletons of coral reefs (the Upper Keys), which thrived in the area during interglacial periods when sea level was higher than at present.

Unique habitats are found on alvars, extremely level expanses of limestone with thin soil mantles. The largest such expanse in Europe is the Stora Alvaret on the island of Öland, Sweden. Another area with large quantities of limestone is the island of Gotland, Sweden. Huge quarries in northwestern Europe, such as those of Mount Saint Peter (Belgium/Netherlands), extend for more than a hundred kilometres.

The world's largest limestone quarry is at Michigan Limestone and Chemical Company in Rogers City, Michigan.

Uses

Limestone is very common in architecture, especially in North America and Europe. Many landmarks across the world, including the Great Pyramid and its associated Complex in Giza, Egypt, are made of limestone. So many buildings in Kingston, Canada were constructed from it that it is nicknamed the 'Limestone City'. On the island of Malta, a variety of limestone called Globigerina limestone was for a long time the only building material available, and is still very frequently used on all types of buildings and sculptures. Limestone is readily available and relatively easy to cut into blocks or more elaborate carving. It is also long-lasting and stands up well to exposure. However, it is a very heavy material, making it impractical for tall buildings, and relatively expensive as a building material.

Limestone was most popular in the late 19th and early 20th centuries. Train stations, banks and other structures from that era are normally made of limestone. Limestone is used as a facade on some skyscrapers, but only in thin plates for covering rather than solid blocks. In the United States, Indiana, most notably the Bloomington area, has long been a source of high quality quarried limestone, called Indiana limestone. Many famous buildings in London are built from Portland limestone.

Limestone was also a very popular building block in the Middle Ages in the areas where it occurred since it is hard, is durable, and commonly occurs in easily accessible surface exposures. Many mediaeval churches and castles in Europe are made of limestone. Beer stone was a popular kind of limestone for mediaeval buildings in southern England.

Limestone and (to a lesser extent) marble are reactive to acid solutions, making acid rain a significant problem to the preservation of artifacts made from this stone. Many limestone statues and building surfaces have suffered severe damage due to acid rain. Acid-based cleaning chemicals can also etch limestone, which should only be cleaned with a neutral or mild alkaline-based cleaner. Other uses include:

- The manufacture of quicklime (calcium oxide) and slaked lime (calcium hydroxide);
- Cement and mortar;
- Pulverized limestone is used as a soil conditioner to neutralize acidic soil conditions;
- Crushed for use as aggregate — the solid base for many roads;
- Geological formations of limestone are among the best petroleum reservoirs;
- As a reagent in desulfurizations;
- Glass making, in some circumstances;

- Added to paper, plastics, paint, tiles, and other materials as both white pigment and a cheap filler.

Toothpaste

Suppression of methane explosions in underground coal mines.

Added to bread and cereals as a source of calcium.

Calcium supplement for poultry (when ground up)

Remineralizing and increasing the alkalinity of purified water to prevent pipe corrosion and to return essential nutrients.

16 Sedimentary Rock

Sedimentary rock is a type of rock that is formed by sedimentation of material at the Earth's surface and within bodies of water. Sedimentation is the collective name for processes that cause mineral and/or organic particles (detritus) to settle and accumulate or minerals to precipitate from a solution. Particles that form a sedimentary rock by accumulating are called sediment. Before being deposited, sediment was formed by weathering and erosion in a source area, and then transported to the place of deposition by water, wind, mass movement or glaciers.

The sedimentary rock cover of the continents of the Earth's crust is extensive, but the total contribution of sedimentary rocks is estimated to be only 5 per cent of the total volume of the crust. Sedimentary rocks are only a thin veneer over a crust consisting mainly of igneous and metamorphic rocks.

Sedimentary rocks are deposited in strata that form a structure called bedding. The study of sedimentary rocks and rock strata provides information about the subsurface that is useful for civil engineering, for example in the construction of roads, houses, tunnels canals or other constructions. Sedimentary rocks are also important sources of natural resources like coal, fossil fuels, drinking water or ores.

The study of the sequence of sedimentary rock strata is the main source for scientific knowledge about the Earth's history, including palaeogeography, paleoclimatology and the history of life.

The scientific discipline that studies the properties and origin of sedimentary rocks is called sedimentology. Sedimentology is both part of geology and physical geography and overlaps partly with other disciplines in the Earth sciences, such as pedology, geomorphology, geo-chemistry or structural geology.

Clastic sedimentary rocks are composed of discrete fragments or clasts of materials derived from other minerals. They are composed largely of quartz with other common minerals including feldspar, amphiboles, clay minerals, and sometimes more exotic igneous and metamorphic minerals.

Clastic sedimentary rocks, such as limestone or sandstone, were formed from rocks that have been broken down into fragments by weathering, which then have been transported and deposited elsewhere.

Clastic sedimentary rocks may be regarded as falling along a scale of grain size, with shale being the finest with particles less than 0.002 mm, siltstone being a little bigger with particles between 0.002 to 0.063 mm, and sandstone being coarser still with grains 0.063 to 2 mm, and conglomerates and breccias being more coarse with grains 2 to 263 mm. Breccia has sharper particles, while conglomerate is categorized by its rounded particles. Particles bigger than 263 mm are termed *blocks* (angular) or *boulders* (rounded). *Lutite, Arenite* and *Rudite* are general terms for sedimentary rock with clay/silt-, sand- or conglomerate/breccia-sized particles.

The classification of clastic sedimentary rocks is complex because there are many variables involved. Particle size (both the average size and range of sizes of the particles), composition of the particles (in sandstones, this includes quartz arenites, arkoses, and lithic sandstones), the cement, and the matrix (the name given to the smaller particles present in the spaces between larger grains) must all be taken into consideration.

Shales, which consist mostly of clay minerals, are generally further classified on the basis of composition and bedding. Coarser clastic sedimentary rocks are classified according to their particle size and composition. Orthoquartzite is a very pure quartz sandstone; arkose is a sandstone with quartz and abundant feldspar; greywacke is a sandstone with quartz, clay, feldspar, and metamorphic rock fragments present, which was formed from the sediments carried by turbidity currents.

All rocks disintegrate when exposed to mechanical and chemical weathering at the Earth's surface.

Lower Antelope Canyon was carved out of the surrounding sandstone by both mechanical weathering and chemical weathering. Wind, sand, and water from flash flooding are the primary weathering agents.

Mechanical Weathering

Mechanical weathering is the breakdown of rock into particles without producing changes in the chemical composition of the minerals in the rock. Ice is the most important agent of mechanical weathering. Water percolates into cracks and fissures within the rock, freezes, and expands. The force exerted by the expansion is sufficient to widen cracks and break off pieces of rock. Heating and cooling of the rock, and the resulting expansion and contraction, also aids the process. Mechanical weathering contributes further to the breakdown of rock by increasing the surface area exposed to chemical agents.

Chemical Weathering

Chemical weathering is the breakdown of rock by chemical reaction. In this process the minerals within the rock are changed into particles that can be easily carried away. Air and water are both involved in many complex chemical reactions. The minerals in igneous rocks may be unstable under normal atmospheric conditions, those formed at higher temperatures being more readily attacked than those which formed at lower temperatures. Igneous rocks are commonly attacked by water, particularly acid or alkaline solutions, and all of the common igneous rock forming minerals (with the exception of quartz which is very resistant) are changed in this way into clay minerals and chemicals in solution.

Rock particles in the form of clay, silt, sand, and gravel are transported by the agents of erosion (usually water, and less frequently, ice and wind) to new locations and redeposited in layers, generally at a lower elevation.

These agents reduce the size of the particles, sort them by size, and then deposit them in new locations. The sediments dropped by streams and rivers form alluvial fans, flood plains, deltas, and on the bottom of lakes and the sea floor. The wind may move large amounts of sand and other smaller particles. Glaciers transport and deposit great quantities of usually unsorted rock material as till.

These deposited particles eventually become compacted and cemented together, forming clastic sedimentary rocks. Such rocks contain inert minerals which are resistant to mechanical and chemical breakdown such as quartz. Quartz is one of the most mechanically and chemically resistant minerals. Highly weathered sediments can contain several heavy and stable minerals, best illustrated by the ZTR index.

Organic

Organic sedimentary rocks contain materials generated by living organisms, and include carbonate minerals created by organisms, such as corals, mollusks, and foraminifera, which cover the ocean floor with layers of calcium carbonate which can later form limestone. Other examples include stromatolites, the flint nodules found in chalk (which is itself a biochemical sedimentary rock, a form of limestone), and coal and oil shale (derived from the remains of tropical plants and subjected to heat).

Chemical

Chemical sedimentary rocks form when minerals in solution become supersaturated and precipitate. In marine environments, this is a method for the formation of limestone. Another common environment in which chemical sedimentary rocks form is a body of water that is evaporating. Evaporation decreases the amount of water without decreasing the amount of dissolved material. Therefore, the dissolved material can become oversaturated and precipitate. Sedimentary rocks from this process can include the evaporite minerals halite (rock salt), sylvite, barite and gypsum.

Formation

Sedimentary rocks are formed when sediment is deposited out of air, ice, wind, gravity, or water flows carrying the particles in suspension. This sediment often formed when weathering and erosion break down a rock into loose material in a source area. The material will then be transported from the source area to the area of deposition. The type of sediment that is transported to a place depends on the geology of the hinterland (the source area of the sediment). However, some sedimentary rocks, like evaporites, are composed of material that formed at the place of deposition. The nature of a sedimentary rock therefore not only depends on sediment supply, but also on the sedimentary depositional environment in which it formed.

Sedimentary Environments

The setting in which a sedimentary rock forms is called the sedimentary environment. Every environment has a characteristic combination of geologic processes and circumstances. The type of sediment that is deposited is not only dependent on the sediment that is transported to a place, but also on the environment itself.

A marine environment means the rock was formed in a sea or ocean. Often, a distinction is made between deep and shallow marine environments. Deep marine usually refers to environments more than 200 m below the water surface. Shallow marine environments exist adjacent to coastlines and can extend out to the boundaries of the continental shelf. The water in such environments has a generally higher energy than that in deep environments, because of wave activity. This means coarser sediment particles can be transported and the deposited sediment can be coarser than in deep environments. When the available sediment is transported from the continent, an alternation of sand, clay and silt will be deposited. When the continent is far away, the amount of such sediment brought in may be small, and biochemical processes will dominate the type of rock that is formed. Especially in warm climates, shallow marine environments far offshore will mainly see the deposition of carbonate rocks. The shallow, warm water is an ideal habitat for many small organisms that build carbonate skeletons. When these organisms die their skeletons sink to the bottom, forming a thick layer of calcareous mud that may lithify into limestone. Warm shallow marine environments also are ideal environments for coral reefs, where the sediment consists mainly of the calcareous skeletons of larger organisms.

In deep marine environments, the water current over the sea bottom is small. Only fine particles can be transported to such places. Typically sediments depositing on the ocean floor are fine clay or small skeletons of micro-organisms. At 4-km depth, the solubility of carbonates increases dramatically (the depth zone where this happens is called the lysocline). Calcareous sediment that sinks below the lysocline will dissolve, so no limestone can be formed below this depth. Skeletons of micro-organisms formed of silica (such as radiolarians) still deposit though. An example of a rock formed out of silica skeletons is radiolarite. When the bottom of the sea has a small inclination, for example at the continental slopes, the sedimentary cover can become unstable, causing turbidity currents. Turbidity currents are sudden disturbances of the normally quite deep marine environment and can cause the geologically speaking instantaneous deposition of large amounts of sediment, such as sand and silt. The rock sequence formed by a turbidity current is called a turbidite.

The coast is an environment dominated by wave action. At the beach, dominantly coarse sediment like sand or gravel is deposited, often mingled with shell fragments. Tidal flats and shoals are places that will sometimes fall dry as a result of the tide. They are often cross-cut by gullies, where the current is strong and the grain size of the deposited sediment is larger. Where along a coast (either the coast of a sea or a lake) rivers enter the body of water, deltas can form. These are large accumulations of sediment transported from the continent to places in front of the mouth of the river. Deltas are dominantly composed of clastic sediment.

A sedimentary rock formed on the land has a continental sedimentary environment. Examples of continental environments are lagoons, lakes, swamps, floodplains and alluvial fans. In the quite water of swamps, lakes and lagoons, fine sediment is deposited, mingled with organic material from dead plants and animals. In rivers, the energy of the water is much higher and the transported material consists of clastic sediment. Besides transport by water, sediment can in continental environments also be transported by wind or glaciers. Sediment transported by wind is called aeolian and is always very well sorted, while sediment transported by a glacier is called glacial and is characterized by very poor sorting.

Sedimentary Facies

Sedimentary environments usually exist alongside each other in certain natural successions. A beach, where sand and gravel is deposited, will usually be bounded by a deeper marine environment a little offshore, where finer sediments are deposited at the same time. Behind the beach, there can be dunes (where the dominant deposition is well sorted sand) or a lagoon (where fine clay and organic material is deposited). Every sedimentary environment has its own characteristic deposits. The typical rock formed in a certain environment is called its sedimentary facies. When sedimentary strata accumulate through time, the environment can shift, forming a change in facies in the subsurface at one location. On the other hand, when a rock layer with a certain age is followed laterally, the lithology (the type of rock) and facies will eventually change.

Facies can be distinguished in a number of ways: the most common ways are by the lithology (for example: limestone, siltstone or sandstone) or by fossil content. Coral for example only lives in warm and shallow marine environments and fossils of coral are thus typical for shallow marine facies. Facies determined by lithology are called lithofacies; facies determined by fossils are biofacies.

Sedimentary environments can shift their geographical positions through time. Coastlines can shift in the direction of the sea when the sea level drops, when the surface rises due to tectonic forces in the Earth's crust or when a river forms a large delta. In the subsurface, such geographic shifts of sedimentary environments of the past are recorded in shifts in sedimentary facies. This means that sedimentary facies can change either parallel or perpendicular to an imaginary layer of rock with a fixed age, a phenomenon described by Walther's facies rule.

The situation in which coastlines move in the direction of the continent is called transgression. In the case of transgression, deeper marine facies will be deposited over shallower facies, a succession called onlap. Regression is the situation in which a coastline moves in the direction of the sea. With regression, shallower facies will be deposited on top of deeper facies, a situation called offlap.

The facies of all rocks of a certain age can be plotted on a map to give an overview of the palaeogeography. A sequence of maps for different ages can give an insight in the development of the regional geography.

Sedimentary Basins

Places where large-scale sedimentation takes place are called sedimentary basins. The amount of sediment that can be deposited in a basin depends on the depth of the basin, the so called accommodation space. Depth, shape and size of a basin depend on tectonics, movements within the Earth's lithosphere. Where the lithosphere moves upward (tectonic uplift), land will in due course rise above sea level, so that and erosion will remove material and the area becomes a source for new sediment. At places where the lithosphere moves downward (tectonic subsidence) a basin will form where sedimentation can take place. When the lithosphere keeps subsiding, new accommodation space keeps being created.

A type of basin formed by the moving apart of two pieces of a continent is called a rift basin. Rift basins are elongated, narrow and deep basins. Due to divergent movement, the lithosphere is stretched and thinned, so that the hot asthenosphere will rise and heat the overlying rift basin. Apart from continental sediments, rift basins normally also have part of their infill consisting of volcanic deposits. When the basin grows due to continued stretching of the lithosphere, the rift will grow and the sea can enter, forming marine deposits.

When a piece of lithosphere that was heated and stretched cools again, its density will rise, causing isostatic subsidence. If this subsidence continues long enough the basin is called a sag basin. Examples of sag basins are the regions along passive continental margins, but sag basins can also be found in the interior of continents. In sag basins, the extra weight of the newly deposited sediments is enough to keep the subsidence going in a vicious circle. The total thickness of the sedimentary infill in a sag basins can thus exceed 10-km.

A third type of basin exists along convergent plate boundaries - places where one tectonic plate moves under another into the asthenosphere. The subducting plate will bend and as a result a fore-arc basin forms in front of the overriding plate, an elongated, deep asymmetric basin. Fore-arc basins are filled with deep marine deposits and thick sequences of turbidites. Such infill is called flysch. When the convergent movement of the two plates results in continental collision, the basin will become shallower and develop into a foreland basin. At the same time, tectonic uplift forms a mountain belt in the overriding plate, from which large amounts of material are eroded and transported to the basin. Such erosional material of a growing mountain chain is called molasse and has either a shallow marine or a continental facies.

At the same time, the growing weight of the mountain belt can cause isostatic subsidence in the area of the overriding plate on the other side to the mountain belt. The basin type resulting from this subsidence is called a back-arc basin and is usually filled by shallow marine deposits and molasse.

Influence of Astronomical Cycles

In many cases facies changes and other lithological features in sequences of sedimentary rock have a cyclic nature. This cyclic nature was caused by cyclic changes in sediment supply and the sedimentary environment. Most of these cyclic changes are caused by astronomic cycles. Short astronomic cycles can be the difference between the tides or the spring tide every two weeks. On a larger time-scale, cyclic changes in climate and sea level are caused by Milankovitch cycles: cyclic changes in the orientation and/or position of the Earth's rotational axis and orbit around the Sun. There are a number of Milankovitch cycles known, lasting between 10,000 and 2,00,000 years.

Relatively small changes in the orientation of the Earth's axis or length of the seasons can be a major influence on the Earth's climate. An example are the ice ages of the past 2.6 million years (the Quaternary period), which are assumed to have been caused by astronomic cycles. Climate change can influence the global sea level (and thus the amount of accommodation space in sedimentary basins) and sediment supply from a certain region. Eventually, small changes in astronomic parameters can cause large changes in sedimentary environment and sedimentation.

Sedimentation Rates

The rate at which sediment is deposited differs depending on the location. A channel in a tidal flat can see the deposition of a few metres of sediment in one day, while on the deep ocean floor each year only a few millimetres of sediment accumulate. A distinction can be made between normal sedimentation and sedimentation caused by catastrophic processes. The latter category includes all kinds of sudden exceptional processes like mass movements, rock slides or flooding. Catastrophic processes can see the sudden deposition of a large amount of sediment at once. In some sedimentary environments, most of the total column of sedimentary rock was formed by catastrophic processes, even though the environment is usually a quiet place. Other sedimentary environments are dominated by normal, ongoing sedimentation.

In some sedimentary environments, sedimentation only occurs in some places. In a desert, for example, the wind will deposit siliciclastic material (sand or silt) in some spots, or catastrophic flooding of a wadi can see the sudden deposition of large quantities of detrital material, but in most places eolian erosion dominates. The amount of sedimentary rock that forms is not only dependent on the amount of supplied material, but also on how well the material consolidates. Most deposited sediment will shortly after deposition be removed by erosion.

Diagenesis

Pressure solution at work in a clastic rock. While material dissolves at places where grains are in contact, material crystallizes from the solution (as cement) in open pore spaces. This means there is a net flow of material from areas under high stress to those under low stress. As a result, the rock becomes more compact and harder. Loose sand can become sandstone in this way.

The term diagenesis is used to describe all the chemical, physical, and biological changes, including cementation, undergone by a sediment after its initial deposition, exclusive of surface weathering. Some of these processes cause the sediment to consolidate: a compact, solid substance forms out of loose material. Young sedimentary rocks, especially those of Quaternary age (the most recent period of the geologic time scale) are often still unconsolidated. As sediment deposition builds up, the overburden (or lithostatic) pressure rises and a process known as lithification takes place.

Sedimentary rocks are often saturated with seawater or groundwater, in which minerals can dissolve or from which minerals can precipitate. Precipitating minerals reduce the pore space in a rock, a process called cementation. Due to the decrease in pore space, the original connate fluids are expelled. The precipitated minerals form a cement and make the rock more compact and competent. In this way, loose clasts in a sedimentary rock can become 'glued' together.

When sedimentation continues, an older rock layer becomes buried deeper as a result. The lithostatic pressure in the rock will increase due to the weight of the overlying sedimentary burden. This causes compaction, a process in which grains will reorganize themselves by mechanical means. Compaction is for example an important diagenetic process in clay, which can initially consist of 60 per cent water. During compaction, this interstitial water is pressed out of the rock. Compaction can also be due to chemical processes, such as pressure solution. Pressure solution means material is going into solution at areas under high stress. The dissolved material precipitates again in open pore spaces, which menas there is a nett flow of material into the pores. However, in some cases a certain mineral will dissolve and not precipitate again. This process is called leaching and will increase the pore space in the rock.

Some biochemical processes, like the activity of bacteria, can affect minerals in a rock and are therefore seen as part of diagenesis. Fungi and plants (by there roots) and various other organisms that live beneath the surface can also influence diagenesis.

Burial of rocks due to ongoing sedimentation will lead to an increase in pressure and temperature, which stimulates certain chemical reactions. An example is the reactions by which organic material becomes lignite or coal. When temperature and pressure increase still further, the realm of diagenesis makes way for metamorphism, the process which forms a metamorphic rock.

PROPERTIES

Colour

The colour of a sedimentary rock is often mostly determined by iron, an element which has two major oxides: iron(II) oxide and iron(III) oxide. Iron(II) oxide only forms under anoxic circumstances and gives the rock a grey or greenish colour. Iron(III) oxide is often in the form of the mineral hematite and gives the rock a reddish to brownish colour. In arid continental climates rocks are in direct contact with the atmosphere, and oxidation is an important process, giving the rock a red or orange colour. Thick sequences of red sedimentary rocks formed in arid climates are called red beds. However, a red colour does not necessarily mean the rock formed in a continental environment or arid climate.

The presence of organic material can colour a rock black or grey. Organic material is in nature formed from dead organisms, mostly plants. Normally such material will eventually decay by oxidation or the activity of bacteria. Under anoxic circumstances however organic material cannot decay and a dark sediment, rich in organic material forms. This can for example be the case at the bottom of deep seas and lakes. There is little current in the water in such environments, so that oxygen from surface waters will not be brought down and the deposited sediment will normally be a fine dark clay. Dark rocks rich in organic material are therefore often shales.

Texture

The size, form and orientation of clasts or minerals in a rock is called its texture. The texture is a small-scale property of a rock, but determined many of its large-scale properties, such as the density, porosity or permeabililty.

Clastic rocks have a 'clastic texture', which means they consist of clasts. The 3D orientation of these clasts is called the fabric of the rock. Between the clasts the rock can be composed of a matrix or a cement (the latter can consist of crystals of one or more precipitated minerals). The size and form of clasts can be used to determine the amount and direction of current in the sedimentary environment where the rock was formed. Fine calcareous mud will only settle in quiet water, while gravel can only deposited by water with large currents. The grain size of a rock is usually expressed with the Wentworth scale, though alternative scales are used sometimes. The grain size can be expressed as a diameter or a volume, and is always an average value — a rock is composed of clasts with different sizes. The statistical distribution of grain sizes is different for different rock types and is described in a property called the sorting of the rock. When all clasts are more or less of the same size, the rock is called 'well-sorted', when there is a large spread in grain size, the rock is called 'poorly sorted'.

The form of clasts can reflect the origin of the rock. Coquina, a rock composed of clasts of broken shells, can only form in energetic water. The form of a clast can be described by using four parameters:

- *'surface texture'* describes the amount of small-scale relief of the surface of a grain which is too small to have influence on the general shape;
- *'rounding'* describes the general smoothness of the shape of a grain;
- *'sphericity'* describes the degree in with the grain approaches a sphere; and
- *'grain form'* is used to describe the 3D shape of the grain.

Chemical sedimentary rocks have a non-clastic texture, consisting entirely of crystals. To describe such a texture only the average size of the crystals and the fabric are necessary.

Mineralogy

Most sedimentary rocks contain either quartz (especially siliciclastic rocks) or calcite (especially carbonate rocks). In contrast with igneous and metamorphic rocks, a sedimentary rocks usually contains very few different major minerals. However, the origin of the minerals in a sedimentary rock is often more complex than those in an igneous rock. Minerals in a sedimentary rock can have formed by precipitation during sedimentation or diagenesis. In the second case, the mineral precipitate can have grown over an older generation of cement. A complex diagenetic history can be studied by optical mineralogy, using a petrographic microscope.

Carbonate rocks dominantly consist of carbonate minerals like calcite, aragonite or dolomite. Both cement and clasts (including fossils and ooids) of a carbonate rock can consist of carbonate minerals. The mineralogy of a clastic rock is determined by the supplied material from the source area, the manner of transport to the place of deposition and the stability of a particular mineral. The stability of the major rock forming minerals (their resistance to weathering) is expressed by Bowen's reaction series. In this series, quartz is most stable, followed by feldspar, micas and other less stable minerals that will only be present when little weathering occurred.The amount of weathering depends mainly on the distance to the source area, the local climate and the time it took for the sediment to be transported there. In most sedimentary rocks, mica, feldspar and less stable minerals will have reacted to clay minerals like kaolinite, illite or smectite.

Primary Sedimentary Structures

Structures in sedimentary rocks can be divided in 'primary' structures (formed during deposition) and 'secondary' structures (formed after deposition). Unlike textures, structures are always large-scale features that can easily be studied in the field. Sedimentary structures can tell something about the sedimentary environment or can serve to tell which side was originally facing up in case sedimentary layers have been tilted or overturned by tectonics.

Sedimentary rocks are laid down in layers called beds or strata. A bed is defined as a layer of rock that has a uniform lithology and texture. Beds form by the deposition of layers of sediment on top of each other. The sequence of beds that characterizes sedimentary rocks is called bedding Single beds can be a couple of centimetres to several meters thick. Finer, less pronounced layers are called laminae and the structure it forms in a rock is called lamination. Laminae are usually less than a few centimetres thick. Though bedding and lamination are often originally horizontal in nature, this is not always the case. In some environments, beds are deposited at a (usually small) angle.

Sometimes multiple sets of layers with different orientations exist in the same rock, a structure called cross-bedding. Cross-bedding forms when small-scale erosion occurs during deposition, cutting off part of the beds. Newer beds will then form at an angle with older ones.

The opposite of cross-bedding is parallel lamination, where all sedimentary layering is parallel. With laminations, differences are generally caused by cyclic changes in the sediment supply, caused for example by seasonal changes in rainfall, temperature or biochemical activity. Laminae which represent seasonal changes (like tree rings) are called varves. Some rocks have no lamination at all, their structural character is called massive bedding.

Graded bedding is a structure in which beds with a smaller grain size occur on top of beds with larger grains. This structure forms when fast flowing water stops flowing. Larger, heavier clasts in suspension will settle first; smaller clasts follow later. Though graded bedding can form in many different environments, it is characteristic for turbidity currents.

The bedform (the surface of a particular bed) can be indicative for a particular sedimentary environment too. Examples of bed forms are scour marks, tool marks and ripple marks. Scour marks are hollow traces in the surface where sediment particles were taken into suspension by the flow. Tool marks are tracks of larger clasts rolling over the sedimentary surface in the direction of the flow. Both are often elongated structures and can be used to establish the direction of the flow during deposition.

Ripple marks also form in flowing water. There are two types: asymmetric wave ripples and symmetric current ripples. Environments where the current is in one direction, such as rivers, produce asymmetric ripples. The longer flank of such ripples is oriented opposite to the direction of the current. Wave ripples occur in environments where currents occur in all directions, such as tidal flats.

Another type of bed form are mud cracks, caused by the dehydration of sediment that occasionally comes above the water surface. Such structures are commonly found at tidal flats or point bars along rivers.

Fossils

Sedimentary rocks are the only type of rock that can contain fossils, the remains or imprints of dead organisms. In nature, dead organisms are usually quickly removed by scavengers, bacteria, rotting and erosion. In some exceptional circumstances a carcass is fossilized because these natural processes are unable to work. The chance of fossilisation is higher when the sedimentation rate is high (so that a carcass is quickly buried), in anoxic environments (where little bacterial activity exists) or when the organism had a particularly hard skeleton. Larger, well-preserved fossils are relatively rare. Most sedimentary rocks contains fossils, though with many the fact only becomes apparent when studied under a microscope (microfossils) or with a loupe.

Fossils can both be the direct remains or imprints of organisms and their skeletons. Most commonly preserved are the harder parts of organisms such as bones, shells, woody tissue of plants. Soft tissue has a much smaller chance of being preserved and fossilized and soft tissue of animals older than 40 million years is very rare. Imprints of organisms made while still alive are called trace fossils. Examples are burrows, foot prints, etc.

Being part of a sedimentary rock, fossils will experience the same diagenetic processes as the rock. A shell consisting of calcite can for example dissolve, while a cement of silica then fills the cavity. In the same way, precipitating minerals can fill cavities formerly occupied by blood vessels, vascular tissue or other soft tissues. This preserves the form of the organism but changes the chemical composition, a process called permineralisation. he most common minerals in permineralisation cements are carbonates (especially calcite), forms of amorphous silica (chalcedony, flint, chert) and pyrite. In the case of silica cements, the process is called lithification.

At high pressure and temperature, the organic material of a dead organism will experience chemical reactions in which volatiles like water and carbon dioxide are expulsed. The fossil will in the end consist of a thin layer of pure carbon or its mineralized form, graphite. This form of fossilisation is called carbonisation. It is particularly important for plant fossils. The same process is responsible for the formation of fossil fuels like lignite or coal.

Stratigraphy

That new rock layers are above older rock layers is stated in the principle of superposition. There are usually some gaps in the sequence called unconformities. These represent periods in which no new sediments were being laid down, or when earlier sedimentary layers were raised above sea level and eroded away.

Sedimentary rocks contain important information about the history of the Earth. They contain fossils, the preserved remains of ancient plants and animals. Coal is considered a type of sedimentary rock. The composition of sediments provides us with clues as to the original rock. Differences between successive layers indicate changes to the environment which have occurred over time. Sedimentary rocks can contain fossils because, unlike most igneous and metamorphic rocks, they form at temperatures and pressures that do not destroy fossil remains.

17 Crust

In geology, a crust is the outermost solid shell of a rocky planet or moon, which is chemically distinct from the underlying mantle. The crusts of Earth, our Moon, Mercury, Venus, Mars, Io, and other planetary bodies have been generated largely by igneous processes, and these crusts are richer in incompatible elements than their respective mantles.

Earth's Crust

The crust of the Earth is composed of a great variety of igneous, metamorphic, and sedimentary rocks. The crust is underlain by the mantle. The upper part of the mantle is composed mostly of peridotite, a rock denser than rocks common in the overlying crust. The boundary between the crust and mantle is conventionally placed at the Mohorovicic discontinuity, a boundary defined by a contrast in seismic velocity. Earth's crust occupies less than 1 per cent of Earth's volume.

The oceanic crust of the Earth is different from its continental crust. The oceanic crust is 5 kms (3 miles) to 10 kms (6 miles) thick and is composed primarily of basalt, diabase, and gabbro. The continental crust is typically from 30 kms (20 miles) to 50 kms (30 miles) thick, and is mostly composed of slightly less dense rocks than those of the oceanic crust. Some of these less dense rocks, such as granite, are common in the continental crust but rare to absent in the oceanic crust. Both the continental and oceanic crust 'float' on the mantle. Because the continental crust is thicker, it extends both above and below the oceanic crust, much like a large iceberg floating next to smaller one. (The slightly lighter density of felsic continental rock compared to basaltic ocean rock also contributes to the higher relative elevation of the top of the continental crust.) Because the top of the continental crust is above that of the oceanic, water runs off the continents and collects above the oceanic crust. The continental crust and the oceanic crust are sometimes called sial and sima respectively. Due to the change in velocity of seismic waves it is believed that on continents at a certain depth sial becomes close in its physical properties to sima and the dividing line is called Conrad discontinuity.

The temperature of the crust increases with depth, reaching values typically in the range from about 200 °C (392 °F) to 400 °C (752 °F) at the boundary with the underlying mantle. The crust and underlying relatively rigid mantle make up the lithosphere. Because of convection in the underlying plastic (although non-molten) upper mantle and asthenosphere, the lithosphere is broken into tectonic plates that move. The temperature increases by as much as 30 °C (about 50 °F) for every kilometer locally in the upper part of the crust, but the geothermal gradient is smaller in deeper crust.

Partly by analogy to what is known about our Moon, Earth is considered to have differentiated from an aggregate of planetesimals into its core, mantle and crust within about 100 million years of the formation of the planet, 4.6 billion years ago. The primordial crust was very thin, and was probably recycled by much more vigorous plate tectonics and destroyed by significant asteroid impacts, which were much more common in the early stages of the solar system.

The Earth has probably always had some form of basaltic crust, but the age of the oldest oceanic crust today is only about 200 million years. In contrast, the bulk of the continental crust is much older. The oldest continental crustal rocks on Earth have ages in the range from about 3.7 to 4.28 billion years and have been found in the Narryer Gneiss Terrane in Western Australia, in the Acasta Gneiss in the Northwest Territories on the Canadian Shield, and on other cratonic regions such as those on the Fennoscandian Shield. A few zircons with ages as great as 4.3 billion years have been found in the Narryer Gneiss Terrane.

The average age of the current Earth's continental crust has been estimated to be about 2.0 billion years. Most crustal rocks formed before 2.5 billion years ago are located in cratons. Such old continental crust and the underlying mantle lithosphere are less dense than elsewhere in the earth and so are not readily destroyed by subduction. Formation of new continental crust is linked to periods of intense orogeny or mountain building; these periods coincide with the formation of the supercontinents such as Rodinia, Pangaea and Gondwana. The crust forms in part by aggregation of island arcs including granite and metamorphic fold belts, and it is preserved in part by depletion of the underlying mantle to form buoyant lithospheric mantle.

Composition of the Continental Crust

The continental crust has an average composition similar to that of the igneous rock, andesite. The composition tabulated below and the following discussion are based largely on the summary by Rudnick and Gao (2003). Continental crust is enriched in incompatible elements compared to the basaltic ocean crust and much enriched compared to the underlying mantle. Although the continental crust comprises only about 0.6 weight per cent of the silicate Earth, it contains 20 per cent to 70 per cent of the incompatible elements.

Earth

Earth (or the Earth) is the third planet from the Sun, and the fifth-largest of the eight planets in the Solar System. It is also the largest, most massive, and densest of the Solar System's four terrestrial planets. It is sometimes referred to as the World, the Blue Planet or *Terra*.

Home to millions of species, including humans, Earth is the only place in the Universe where life is known to exist. The planet formed 4.54 billion years ago, and life appeared on its surface within a billion years. Since then, Earth's biosphere has significantly altered the atmosphere and other abiotic conditions on the planet, enabling the proliferation of aerobic organisms as well as the formation of the ozone layer which, together with Earth's magnetic field, blocks harmful radiation, permitting life on land. The physical properties of the Earth, as well as its geological history and orbit, have allowed life to persist during this period. The world is expected to continue supporting life for another 1.5 billion years, after which the rising luminosity of the Sun will eliminate the biosphere.

Earth's outer surface is divided into several rigid segments, or tectonic plates, that gradually migrate across the surface over periods of many millions of years. About 71 per cent of the surface is covered with salt-water oceans, the remainder consisting of continents and islands; liquid water, necessary for all known life, is not known to exist on any other planet's surface. Earth's interior remains active, with a thick layer of relatively solid mantle, a liquid outer core that generates a magnetic field, and a solid iron inner core.

Earth interacts with other objects in outer space, including the Sun and the Moon. At present, Earth orbits the Sun once for every roughly 366.26 times it rotates about its axis. This is a sidereal year, which is equal to 365.26 solar days. The Earth's axis of rotation is tilted 23.4° away from the perpendicular to its orbital plane, producing seasonal variations on the planet's surface with a period of one tropical year (365.24 solar days). Earth's only known natural satellite, the Moon, which began orbiting it about 4.53 billion years ago, provides ocean tides, stabilizes the axial tilt and gradually slows the planet's rotation. Between approximately 4.1 and 3.8 billion years ago, asteroid impacts during the Late Heavy Bombardment caused significant changes to the surface environment.

Both the mineral resources of the planet, as well as the products of the biosphere, contribute resources that are used to support a global human population. The inhabitants are grouped into about 200 independent sovereign states, which interact through diplomacy, travel, trade and military action. Human cultures have developed many views of the planet, including personification as a deity, a belief in a flat Earth or in Earth being the center of the universe, and a modern perspective of the world as an integrated environment that requires stewardship.

Scientists have been able to reconstruct detailed information about the planet's past. The earliest dated Solar System material is dated to 4.5672 ± 0.0006 billion years ago, and by 4.54 billion years ago (within an uncertainty of 1%) the Earth and the other planets in the Solar System formed out of the solar nebula — a disk-shaped mass of dust and gas left over from the formation of the Sun. This assembly of the Earth through accretion was largely completed within 10-20 million years. Initially molten, the outer layer of the planet Earth cooled to form a solid crust when water began accumulating in the atmosphere. The Moon formed shortly thereafter, 4.53 billion years ago.

The current consensus model for the formation of the Moon is the giant impact hypothesis, in which the Moon formed as a result of a Mars-sized object (sometimes called Theia) with about 10 per cent of the Earth's mass impacting the Earth in a glancing blow. In this model, some of this object's mass would have merged with the Earth and a portion would have been ejected into space, but enough material would have been sent into orbit to form the Moon.

Outgassing and volcanic activity produced the primordial atmosphere. Condensing water vapour, augmented by ice and liquid water delivered by asteroids and the larger proto-planets, comets, and trans-Neptunian objects produced the oceans. The newly-formed Sun was only 70 per cent of its present luminosity, yet evidence shows that the early oceans remained liquid – a contradiction dubbed the faint young Sun paradox. A combination of greenhouse gases and higher levels of solar activity served to raise the Earth's surface temperature, preventing the oceans from freezing over.

Two major models have been proposed for the rate of continental growth: steady growth to the present-day and rapid growth early in Earth history. Current research shows that the second option is most likely, with rapid initial growth of continental crust followed by a long-term steady continental area. On time scales lasting hundreds of millions of years, the surface continually reshaped itself as continents formed and broke up. The continents migrated across the surface, occasionally combining to form a supercontinent. Roughly 750 million years ago (Ma), one of the earliest known supercontinents, Rodinia, began to break apart. The continents later recombined to form Pannotia, 600-540 Ma, then finally Pangaea, which broke apart 180 Ma.

Composition and Structure

Earth is a terrestrial planet, meaning that it is a rocky body, rather than a gas giant like Jupiter. It is the largest of the four solar terrestrial planets, both in terms of size and mass. Of these four planets, Earth also has the highest density, the highest surface gravity, the strongest magnetic field, and fastest rotation. It also is the only terrestrial planet with active plate tectonics.

Shape

The shape of the Earth is very close to that of an oblate spheroid, a sphere squished along the orientation from pole to pole such that there is a bulge around the equator. This bulge results from the rotation of the Earth, and causes the diameter at the equator to be 43 kms larger than the pole to pole diameter. The average diameter of the reference spheroid is about 12,742 kms, which is approximately 40,000 km/p, as the meter was originally defined as 1/10,000,000 of the distance from the equator to the North Pole through Paris, France.

Local topography deviates from this idealized spheroid, though on a global scale, these deviations are very small: Earth has a tolerance of about one part in about 584, or 0.17 per cent, from the reference spheroid, which is less than the 0.22 per cent tolerance allowed in billiard balls. The largest local deviations in the rocky surface of the Earth are Mount Everest (8,848 m above local sea level) and the Mariana Trench (10,911 m below local sea level). Because of the equatorial bulge, the feature farthest from the center of the Earth is Mount Chimborazo in Ecuador.

Chemical Composition

The mass of the Earth is approximately 5.98×10^{24} kg. It is composed mostly of iron (32.1%), oxygen (30.1%), silicon (15.1%), magnesium (13.9%), sulfur (2.9%), nickel (1.8%), calcium (1.5%), and aluminium (1.4%); with the remaining 1.2 per cent consisting of trace amounts of other elements. Due to mass segregation, the core region is believed to be primarily composed of iron (88.8%), with smaller amounts of nickel (5.8%), sulfur (4.5%), and less than 1 per cent trace elements.

The geochemist F.W. Clarke calculated that a little more than 47 per cent of the Earth's crust consists of oxygen. The more common rock constituents of the Earth's crust are nearly all oxides; chlorine, sulfur and fluorine are the only important exceptions to this and their total amount in any rock is usually much less than 1 per cent. The principal oxides are silica, alumina, iron oxides, lime, magnesia, potash and soda. The silica functions principally as an acid, forming silicates, and all the commonest minerals of igneous rocks are of this nature. From a computation based on 1,672 analyses of all kinds of rocks, Clarke deduced that 99.22 per cent were composed of 11 oxides. All the other constituents occur only in very small quantities.

Tectonic Plates

The mechanically rigid outer layer of the Earth, the lithosphere, is broken into pieces called tectonic plates. These plates are rigid segments that move in relation to one another at one of three types of plate boundaries: Convergent boundaries, at which two plates come together, Divergent boundaries, at which two plates are pulled apart, and Transform boundaries, in which two plates slide past one another laterally. Earthquakes, volcanic activity, mountain-building, and oceanic trench formation can occur along these plate boundaries. The tectonic plates ride on top of the asthenosphere, the solid but less-viscous part of the upper mantle that can flow and move along with the plates, and their motion is strongly coupled with patterns convection inside the Earth's mantle.

As the tectonic plates migrate across the planet, the ocean floor is subducted under the leading edges of the plates at convergent boundaries. At the same time, the upwelling of mantle material at divergent boundaries creates mid-ocean ridges. The combination of these processes continually recycles the oceanic crust back into the mantle. Because of this recycling, most of the ocean floor is less than 100 million years in age. The oldest oceanic crust is located in the Western Pacific, and has an estimated age of about 200 million years. By comparison, the oldest dated continental crust is 4030 million years old.

Other notable plates include the Indian Plate, the Arabian Plate, the Caribbean Plate, the Nazca Plate off the west coast of South America and the Scotia Plate in the southern Atlantic Ocean. The Australian Plate fused with Indian Plate between 50 and 55 million years ago. The fastest-moving plates are the oceanic plates, with the Cocos Plate advancing at a rate of 75 mm/yr and the Pacific Plate moving 52-69 mm/yr. At the other extreme, the slowest-moving plate is the Eurasian Plate, progressing at a typical rate of about 21 mm/yr.

Surface

The Earth's terrain varies greatly from place to place. About 70.8 per cent of the surface is covered by water, with much of the continental shelf below sea level. The submerged surface has mountainous features, including a globe-spanning mid-ocean ridge system, as well as undersea volcanoes, oceanic trenches, submarine canyons, oceanic plateaus and abyssal plains. The remaining 29.2 per cent not covered by water consists of mountains, deserts, plains, plateaus, and other geomorphologies.

The planetary surface undergoes reshaping over geological time periods due to the effects of tectonics and erosion. The surface features built up or deformed through plate tectonics are subject to steady weathering from precipitation, thermal cycles, and chemical effects. Glaciation, coastal erosion, the build-up of coral reefs, and large meteorite impacts also act to reshape the landscape.

The continental crust consists of lower density material such as the igneous rocks granite and andesite. Less common is basalt, a denser volcanic rock that is the primary constituent of the ocean floors. Sedimentary rock is formed from the accumulation of sediment that becomes compacted together. Nearly 75 per cent of the continental surfaces are covered by sedimentary rocks, although they form only about 5 per cent of the crust. The third form of rock material found on Earth is metamorphic rock, which is created from the transformation of pre-existing rock types through high pressures, high temperatures, or both. The most abundant silicate minerals on the Earth's surface include quartz, the feldspars, amphibole, mica, pyroxene and olivine. Common carbonate minerals include calcite (found in limestone), aragonite and dolomite.

The pedosphere is the outermost layer of the Earth that is composed of soil and subject to soil formation processes. It exists at the interface of the lithosphere, atmosphere, hydrosphere and biosphere. Currently the total arable land is 13.31 per cent of the land surface, with only 4.71 per cent supporting permanent crops. Close to 40 per cent of the Earth's land surface is presently used for cropland and pasture, or an estimated 1.3×10^7 km^2 of cropland and 3.4×10^7 km^2 of pastureland.

Magnetic Field

The Earth's magnetic field is shaped roughly as a magnetic dipole, with the poles currently located proximate to the planet's geographic poles. According to dynamo theory, the field is generated within the molten outer core region where heat creates convection motions of conducting materials, generating electric currents. These in turn produce the Earth's magnetic field. The convection movements in the core are chaotic in nature, and periodically change alignment. This results in field reversals at irregular intervals averaging a few times every million years. The most recent reversal occurred approximately 7,00,000 years ago.

The field forms the magnetosphere, which deflects particles in the solar wind. The sunward edge of the bow shock is located at about 13 times the radius of the Earth. The collision between the magnetic field and the solar wind forms the Van Allen radiation belts, a pair of concentric, torus-shaped regions of energetic charged particles. When the plasma enters the Earth's atmosphere at the magnetic poles, it forms the aurora.

The Earth provides resources that are exploitable by humans for useful purposes. Some of these are non-renewable resources, such as mineral fuels, that are difficult to replenish on a short time scale.

Large deposits of fossil fuels are obtained from the Earth's crust, consisting of coal, petroleum, natural gas and methane clathrate. These deposits are used by humans both for energy production and as feedstock for chemical production. Mineral ore bodies have also been formed in Earth's crust through a process of Ore genesis, resulting from actions of erosion and plate tectonics. These bodies form concentrated sources for many metals and other useful elements.

The Earth's biosphere produces many useful biological products for humans, including (but far from limited to) food, wood, pharmaceuticals, oxygen, and the recycling of many organic wastes. The land-based ecosystem depends upon topsoil and fresh water, and the oceanic ecosystem depends upon dissolved nutrients washed down from the land. Humans also live on the land by using building materials to construct shelters. In 1993, human use of land is approximately.

Natural and Environmental Hazards

Large areas are subject to extreme weather such as tropical cyclones, hurricanes, or typhoons that dominate life in those areas. Many places are subject to earthquakes, landslides, tsunamis, volcanic eruptions, tornadoes, sinkholes, blizzards, floods, droughts, and other calamities and disasters.

Many localized areas are subject to human-made pollution of the air and water, acid rain and toxic substances, loss of vegetation (overgrazing, deforestation, desertification), loss of wildlife, species extinction, soil degradation, soil depletion, erosion, and introduction of invasive species.

A scientific consensus exists linking human activities to global warming due to industrial carbon dioxide emissions. This is predicted to produce changes such as the melting of glaciers and ice sheets, more extreme temperature ranges, significant changes in weather and a global rise in average sea levels.

18 Plate Tectonics

Plate tectonics (from the Late Latin *tectonicus* a scientific theory which describes the large scale motions of Earth's lithosphere. It is vital for the existence of life on earth because of the role that it plays in the global cycle that maintains the balance of carbon between the biosphere, pedosphere, geosphere, hydrosphere, and atmosphere. A similar process likely takes place on other celestial objects when they are sufficiently similar to Earth. The theory builds on the older concepts of continental drift, developed during the first decades of the 20th century by Alfred Wegener, and seafloor spreading, developed in the 1960s.

The lithosphere is broken up into what are called tectonic plates. In the case of Earth, there are currently seven to eight major (depending on how they are defined) and many minor plates. The lithospheric plates ride on the asthenosphere. These plates move in relation to one another at one of three types of plate boundaries: convergent, or collisional boundaries; divergent boundaries, also called spreading centers; and transform boundaries. Earthquakes, volcanic activity, mountain-building, and oceanic trench formation occur along plate boundaries. The lateral movement of the plates is typically 50-100 mm annually.

Tectonic plates are able to move because the Earth's lithosphere has a higher strength and lower density than the underlying asthenosphere. Their movement is driven by heat dissipation from the mantle. Lateral density variations in the mantle result in convection, which is transferred into tectonic plate motion through some combination of drag, downward suction at the subduction zones, and variations in topography and density of the crust that result in differences in gravitational forces. The relative importance of each of these factors is unclear.

In the late 19th and early 20th centuries, geologists assumed that the Earth's major features were fixed, and that most geologic features such as mountain ranges could be explained by vertical crustal movement, through geosynclinal theory. It was observed as early as 1596 that the opposite coasts of the Atlantic Ocean – or, more precisely, the edges of the continental shelves – have similar shapes and seem to have once fitted together. Since that time many theories were proposed to explain this apparent complementarity, but the assumption of a solid earth made the various proposals difficult to explain.

The discovery of radioactivity and its associated heating properties in 1895 prompted a re-examination of the apparent age of the Earth, since this had previously been estimated by its cooling rate and assumption the Earth's surface radiated like a black body. Those calculations had implied that, even if it started at red heat, the Earth would have dropped to its present temperature in a few tens of millions of years. Armed with the knowledge of a new heat source, scientists realized that the Earth would be much older, and that its core was still sufficiently hot to be liquid.

Plate tectonic theory arose out of the hypothesis of continental drift proposed by Alfred Wegener in 1912 and expanded in his 1915 book "The Origin of Continents and Oceans". He suggested that the present continents once formed a single land mass that drifted apart, thus releasing the continents from the Earth's core and likening them to 'icebergs' of low density granite floating on a sea of denser basalt. But without detailed evidence and a force sufficient to drive the movement, the theory was not generally accepted: the Earth might have a solid crust and a liquid core, but there seemed to be no way that portions of the crust could move around. Later science supported theories proposed by English geologist Arthur Holmes in 1920 that plate junctions might lie beneath the sea and Holmes' 1928 suggestion of convection currents within the mantle as the driving force.

The first evidence that the lithospheric plates did move came with the discovery of variable magnetic field direction in rocks of differing ages, first revealed at a symposium in Tasmania in 1956. Initially theorized as an expansion of the global crust, later collaborations developed the plate tectonic theory, which accounted for spreading as the consequence of new rock upwelling, but avoided the need for an expanding globe by recognizing subduction zones and conservative translation faults. It was at this point that Wegener's theory became generally accepted by the scientific community. Additional work on the association of seafloor spreading and magnetic field reversals by Harry Hess and Ron G. Mason pinpointed the precise mechanism which accounted for new rock upwelling.

Following the recognition of magnetic anomalies defined by symmetric, parallel stripes of similar magnetization on the seafloor on either side of a mid-ocean ridge, plate tectonics quickly became broadly accepted. Simultaneous advances in early seismic imaging techniques in and around Wadati-Benioff zones together with many other geologic observations soon made plate tectonics a theory with extraordinary explanatory and predictive power.

Study of the deep ocean floor was critical to development of the theory; the field of deep sea marine geology accelerated in the 1960s. Correspondingly, plate tectonic theory was developed during the late 1960s and has since been accepted by almost all scientists throughout all geoscientific disciplines. The theory revolutionized the Earth sciences, explaining a diverse range of geological phenomena and their implications in other studies such as paleogeography and paleobiology.

Key Principles

The outer layers of the Earth are divided into lithosphere and asthenosphere. This is based on differences in mechanical properties and in the method for the transfer of heat. Mechanically, the lithosphere is cooler and more rigid, while the asthenosphere is hotter and flows more easily. In terms of heat transfer, the lithosphere loses heat by conduction whereas the asthenosphere also transfers heat by convection and has a nearly adiabatic temperature gradient. This division should not be confused with the chemical subdivision of these same layers into the mantle (comprising both the asthenosphere and the mantle portion of the lithosphere) and the crust: a given piece of mantle may be part of the lithosphere or the asthenosphere at different times, depending on its temperature and pressure.

The key principle of plate tectonics is that the lithosphere exists as separate and distinct *tectonic plates*, which ride on the fluid-like (visco-elastic solid) asthenosphere. Plate motions range up to a typical 10-40 mm/a (Mid-Atlantic Ridge; about as fast as fingernails grow), to about 160 mm/a (Nazca Plate; about as fast as hair grows).

Tectonic plates consist of lithospheric mantle overlain by either of two types of crustal material: oceanic crust (in older texts called *sima* from silicon and magnesium) and continental crust (*sial* from silicon and aluminium). Average oceanic lithosphere is typically 100 km thick its thickness is a function of its age: as time passes, it conductively cools and becomes thicker. Because it is formed at mid-ocean ridges and spreads outwards, its thickness is therefore a function of its distance from the mid-ocean ridge where it was formed. For a typical distance oceanic lithosphere must travel before being subducted, the thickness varies ~6 kms thick at mid-ocean ridges to greater than 100 km at subduction zones; for shorter or longer distances, the subduction zone (and therefore also the mean) thickness becomes smaller or larger, respectively. Typical continental lithosphere is typically ~200 kms thick, though this also varies considerably between basins, mountain ranges, and stable cratonic interiors of continents. The two types of crust also differ in thickness, with continental crust being considerably thicker than oceanic (35 kms vs. 6 kms).

The location where two plates meet is called a *plate boundary*, and plate boundaries are commonly associated with geological events such as earthquakes and the creation of topographic features such as mountains, volcanoes, mid-ocean ridges, and oceanic trenches. The majority of the world's active volcanoes occur along plate boundaries, with the Pacific Plate's Ring of Fire being most active and most widely known.

Tectonic plates can include continental crust or oceanic crust, and many plates contain both. For example, the African Plate includes the continent and parts of the floor of the Atlantic and Indian Oceans. The distinction between oceanic crust and continental crust is based on their modes of formation. Oceanic crust is formed at sea-floor spreading centers, and continental crust is formed through arc volcanism and accretion of terranes through tectonic processes; though some of these terranes may contain ophiolite sequences, which are pieces of oceanic crust, these are considered part of the continent when they exit the standard cycle of formation and spreading centers and subduction beneath continents. Oceanic crust is also denser than continental crust owing to their different compositions. Oceanic crust is denser because it has less silicon and more heavier elements ('mafic') than continental crust ('felsic').

As a result of this density stratification, oceanic crust generally lies below sea level (for example most of the Pacific Plate), while the continental crust buoyantly projects above sea level (see isostasy for explanation of this principle).

Types of Plate Boundaries

Three types of plate boundaries exist, characterized by the way the plates move relative to each other. They are associated with different types of surface phenomena. The different types of plate boundaries are:

- *Transform boundaries* occur where plates slide or, perhaps more accurately, grind past each other along transform faults. The relative motion of the two plates is either sinistral (left side toward the observer) or dextral (right side toward the observer). The San Andreas Fault in California is an example of a transform boundary exhibiting dextral motion.
- *Divergent boundaries* occur where two plates slide apart from each other. Mid-ocean ridges (*e.g.*, Mid-Atlantic Ridge) and active zones of rifting (such as Africa's Great Rift Valley) are both examples of divergent boundaries.
- *Convergent boundaries* (or *active margins*) occur where two plates slide towards each other commonly forming either a subduction zone (if one plate moves underneath the other) or a continental collision (if the two plates contain continental crust). Deep marine trenches are typically associated with subduction zones. The subducting slab contains many hydrous minerals, which release their water on heating; this water then causes the mantle to melt, producing volcanism. Examples of this are the Andes mountain range in South America and the Japanese island arc.

Driving Forces of Plate Motion

Tectonic plates are able to move because of the relative density of oceanic lithosphere and the relative weakness of the asthenosphere. Dissipation of heat from the mantle is acknowledged to be the original source of energy driving plate tectonics. The current view, although it is still a matter of some debate, is that excess density of the oceanic lithosphere sinking in subduction zones is the most powerful source of plate motion. When it forms at mid-ocean ridges, the oceanic lithosphere is initially less dense than the underlying asthenosphere, but it becomes denser with age, as it conductively cools and thickens. The greater density of old lithosphere relative to the underlying asthenosphere allows it to sink into the deep mantle at subduction zones, providing most of the driving force for plate motions. The weakness of the asthenosphere allows the tectonic plates to move easily towards a subduction zone. Although subduction is believed to be the strongest force driving plate motions, it cannot be the only force since there are plates such as the North American Plate which are moving, yet are nowhere being subducted. The same is true for the enormous Eurasian Plate. The sources of plate motion are a matter of intensive research and discussion among earth scientists.

Two and three - dimensional imaging of the Earth's interior shows that there is a laterally varying density distribution throughout the mantle. Such density variations can be material (from rock chemistry), mineral (from variations in mineral structures), or thermal (through thermal expansion and contraction from heat energy). The manifestation of this varying lateral density is mantle convection from buoyancy forces. How mantle convection relates directly and indirectly to the motion of the plates is a matter of ongoing study and discussion in geodynamics. Somehow, this energy must be transferred to the lithosphere in order for tectonic plates to move. There are essentially two types of forces that are thought to influence plate motion: friction and gravity.

FRICTION

Basal Drag

Large scale convection currents in the upper mantle are transmitted through the asthenosphere; motion is driven by friction between the asthenosphere and the lithosphere.

Slab Suction

Local convection currents exert a downward frictional pull on plates in subduction zones at ocean trenches. Slab suction may occur in a geodynamic setting wherein basal tractions continue to act on the plate as it dives into the mantle (although perhaps to a greater extent acting on both the under and upper side of the slab).

Gravitation

Gravitational sliding: Plate motion is driven by the higher elevation of plates at ocean ridges. As oceanic lithosphere is formed at spreading ridges from hot mantle material, it gradually cools and thickens with age (and thus distance from the ridge). Cool oceanic lithosphere is significantly denser than the hot mantle material from which it is derived and so with increasing thickness it gradually subsides into the mantle to compensate the greater load. The result is a slight lateral incline with distance from the ridge axis.

Casually in the geophysical community and more typically in the geological literature in lower education this process is often referred to as 'ridge-push'. This is, in fact, a misnomer as nothing is 'pushing' and tensional features are dominant along ridges. It is more accurate to refer to this mechanism as gravitational sliding as variable topography across the totality of the plate can vary considerably and the topography of spreading ridges is only the most prominent feature. For example:

1. Flexural bulging of the lithosphere before it dives underneath an adjacent plate, for instance, produces a

clear topographical feature that can offset or at least affect the influence of topographical ocean ridges.

2. Mantle plumes impinging on the underside of tectonic plates can drastically alter the topography of the ocean floor.

Slab-pull

Plate motion is partly driven by the weight of cold, dense plates sinking into the mantle at trenches. There is considerable evidence that convection is occurring in the mantle at some scale. The upwelling of material at mid-ocean ridges is almost certainly part of this convection. Some early models of plate tectonics envisioned the plates riding on top of convection cells like conveyor belts. However, most scientists working today believe that the asthenosphere is not strong enough to directly cause motion by the friction of such basal forces. Slab pull is most widely thought to be the greatest force acting on the plates. Recent models indicate that trench suction plays an important role as well. However, it should be noted that the North American Plate, for instance, is nowhere being subducted, yet it is in motion. Likewise the African, Eurasian and Antarctic Plates. The overall driving force for plate motion and its energy source remain subjects of ongoing research.

External Forces

In a study published in the January-February 2006 issue of the *Geological Society of America Bulletin*, a team of Italian and U.S. scientists argued that the westward component of every plate's motion is due to Earth's rotation and the tidal friction of the moon. As the Earth spins eastward beneath the moon, they say, the moon's gravity ever so slightly pulls the Earth's surface layer back westward. It has also been suggested (albeit, controversially) that this observation may also explain why Venus and Mars have no plate tectonics since Venus has no moon, and Mars' moons are too small to have significant tidal effects on Mars. This is not, however, a new argument.

It was originally raised by the 'father' of the plate tectonics hypothesis, Alfred Wegener. It was challenged by the physicist Harold Jeffreys who calculated that the magnitude of tidal friction required would have quickly brought the Earth's rotation to a halt long ago. Many plates are moving north and eastward, and the dominantly westward motion of the Pacific ocean basins is simply from the eastward bias of the Pacific spreading center (which is not a predicted manifestation of such lunar forces). It is argued, however, that relative to the lower mantle, there is a slight westward component in the motions of all the plates.

Relative Significance of Each Mechanism

Plate motion based on Global Positioning System (GPS) satellite data from NASA JPL. Vectors show direction and magnitude of motion.

The actual vector of a plate's motion must necessarily be a function of all the forces acting upon the plate. However, therein remains the problem regarding what degree each process contributes to the motion of each tectonic plate.

The diversity of geodynamic settings and properties of each plate must clearly result in differences in the degree to which such processes are actively driving the plates. One method of dealing with this problem is to consider the relative rate at which each plate is moving and to consider the available evidence of each driving force upon the plate as far as possible.

One of the most significant correlations found is that lithospheric plates attached to downgoing (subducting) plates move much faster than plates not attached to subducting plates. The Pacific plate, for instance, is essentially surrounded by zones of subduction (the so-called Ring of Fire) and moves much faster than the plates of the Atlantic basin, which are attached (perhaps one could say 'welded') to adjacent continents instead of subducting plates. It is thus thought that forces associated with the downgoing plate (slab pull and slab suction) are the driving forces which determine the motion of plates, except for those plates which are not being subducted.

The driving forces of plate motion are, nevertheless, still very active subjects of on-going discussion and research in the geophysical.

Movement

The movement of plates has caused the formation and break-up of continents over time, including occasional formation of a supercontinent that contains most or all of the continents. The supercontinent Rodinia is thought to have formed about 1 billion years ago and to have embodied most or all of Earth's continents, and broken up into eight continents around 600 million years ago. The eight continents later re-assembled into another supercontinent called Pangaea; Pangaea broke up into Laurasia (which became North America and Eurasia) and Gondwana (which became the remaining continents).

Continental Drift

Continental drift was one of many ideas about tectonics proposed in the late 19th and early 20th centuries. The theory has been superseded and the concepts and data have been incorporated within plate tectonics.

By 1915, Alfred Wegener was making serious arguments for the idea in the first edition of 'The Origin of Continents and Oceans'. In that book, he noted how the east coast of South America and the west coast of Africa looked as if they were once attached. Wegener wasn't the first to note this (Abraham Ortelius, Francis Bacon, Benjamin Franklin, Snider-Pellegrini, Roberto Mantovani and Frank Bursley Taylor preceded him), but he was the first to marshal significant fossil and paleo-topographical and climatological evidence to support this simple observation (and was supported in this by researchers such as Alex du Toit). However, his ideas were not taken seriously by many geologists, who pointed out that there was no apparent mechanism for continental drift. Specifically, they did not see how continental rock could plow through the much denser rock that makes up oceanic crust. Wegener could not explain the force that drove continental drift.

Wegener's vindication did not come until after his death in 1930. In 1947, a team of scientists led by Maurice Ewing utilizing the Woods Hole Oceanographic Institution's research vessel *Atlantis* and an array of instruments, confirmed the existence of a rise in the central Atlantic Ocean, and found that the floor of the seabed beneath the layer of sediments consisted of basalt, not the granite which is the main constituent of continents. They also found that the oceanic crust was much thinner than continental crust. All these new findings raised important and intriguing questions.

Beginning in the 1950s, scientists including Harry Hess and Victor Vacquier, using magnetic instruments (magnetometers) adapted from airborne devices developed during World War II to detect submarines, began recognizing odd magnetic variations across the ocean floor. This finding, though unexpected, was not entirely surprising because it was known that basalt — the iron-rich, volcanic rock making up the ocean floor — contains a strongly magnetic mineral (magnetite) and can locally distort compass readings. This distortion was recognized by Icelandic mariners as early as the late 18th century. More important, because the presence of magnetite gives the basalt measurable magnetic properties, these newly discovered magnetic variations provided another means to study the deep ocean floor. When newly formed rock cools, such magnetic materials recorded the Earth's magnetic field at the time.

As more and more of the seafloor was mapped during the 1950s, the magnetic variations turned out not to be random or isolated occurrences, but instead revealed recognizable patterns. When these magnetic patterns were mapped over a wide region, the ocean floor showed a zebra-like pattern. Alternating stripes of magnetically different rock were laid out in rows on either side of the mid-ocean ridge: one stripe with normal polarity and the adjoining stripe with reversed polarity. The overall pattern, defined by these alternating bands of normally and reversely polarized rock, became known as magnetic striping.

When the rock strata of the tips of separate continents are very similar it suggests that these rocks were formed in the same way, implying that they were joined initially. For instance, some parts of Scotland and Ireland contain rocks very similar to those found in Newfoundland and New Brunswick. Furthermore, the Caledonian Mountains of Europe and parts of the Appalachian Mountains of North America are very similar in structure and lithology.

Floating Continents

The prevailing concept was that there were static shells of strata under the continents. It was observed early that although granite existed on continents, seafloor seemed to be composed of denser basalt. It was apparent that a layer of basalt underlies continental rocks.

However, based upon abnormalities in plumb line deflection by the Andes in Peru, Pierre Bouguer deduced that less-dense mountains must have a downward projection into the denser layer underneath. The concept that mountains had "roots" was confirmed by George B. Airy a hundred years later during study of Himalayan gravitation, and seismic studies detected corresponding density variations.

By the mid-1950s the question remained unresolved of whether mountain roots were clenched in surrounding basalt or were floating like an iceberg.

In 1958 the Australian geologist Samuel Warren Carey published an essay the tectonic approach to continental drift in support of the expanding earth model.

Plate Tectonic Theory

Significant progress was made in the 1960s, and was prompted by a number of discoveries, most notably of the Mid-Atlantic ridge. The most significant paper was the 1962 publication by American geologist Harry Hammond Hess (Robert S. Dietz published the same idea one year earlier in *Nature*. However, priority belongs to Hess, since he had already distributed an unpublished manuscript of his 1962 article by 1960). Hess suggested that instead of continents moving *through* oceanic crust (as was suggested by continental drift) that an ocean basin and its adjoining continent moved together on the same crustal unit, or plate. In the same year, Robert R. Coats of the U.S. Geological Survey described the main features of island arc subduction in the Aleutian Islands. His paper, though little-noted (and even ridiculed) at the time, has since been called 'seminal' and 'prescient'. In 1967, W. Jason Morgan proposed that the Earth's surface consists of 12 rigid plates that move relative to each other. Two months later, in 1968, Xavier Le Pichon published a complete model based on 6 major plates with their relative motions.

Explanation of Magnetic Striping

The discovery of magnetic striping and the stripes being symmetrical around the crests of the mid-ocean ridges suggested a relationship. In 1961, scientists began to theorise that mid-ocean ridges mark structurally weak zones where the ocean floor was being ripped in two lengthwise along the ridge crest. New magma from deep within the Earth rises easily through these weak zones and eventually erupts along the crest of the ridges to create new oceanic crust. This process, later called seafloor spreading, operating over many millions of years continues to form new ocean floor all across the 50,000 km-long system of mid-ocean ridges. This hypothesis was supported by several lines of evidence:

- at or near the crest of the ridge, the rocks are very young, and they become progressively older away from the ridge crest;
- the youngest rocks at the ridge crest always have present-day (normal) polarity;
- stripes of rock parallel to the ridge crest alternated in magnetic polarity (normal-reversed-normal, etc.), suggesting that the Earth's magnetic field has reversed many times.

By explaining both the zebralike magnetic striping and the construction of the mid-ocean ridge system, the seafloor spreading hypothesis quickly gained converts and represented another major advance in the development of the plate-tectonics theory. Furthermore, the oceanic crust now came to be appreciated as a natural 'tape recording' of the history of the reversals in the Earth's magnetic field.

Subduction Discovered

A profound consequence of seafloor spreading is that new crust was, and is now, being continually created along the oceanic ridges. This idea found great favor with some scientists, most notably S. Warren Carey, who claimed that the shifting of the continents can be simply explained by a large increase in size of the Earth since its formation. However, this so-called 'Expanding Earth theory' hypothesis was unsatisfactory because its supporters could offer no convincing mechanism to produce a significant expansion of the Earth. Certainly there is no evidence that the moon has expanded in the past 3 billion years. Still, the question remained: how can new crust be continuously added along the oceanic ridges without increasing the size of the Earth?

This question particularly intrigued Harry Hess, a Princeton University geologist and a Naval Reserve Rear Admiral, and Robert S. Dietz, a scientist with the U.S. Coast and Geodetic Survey who first coined the term *seafloor spreading*. Dietz and Hess were among the small handful who really understood the broad implications of sea floor spreading. If the Earth's crust was expanding along the oceanic ridges, Hess reasoned, it must be shrinking elsewhere. He suggested that new oceanic crust continuously spreads away from the ridges in a conveyor belt-like motion. Many millions of years later, the oceanic crust eventually descends into the oceanic trenches — very deep, narrow canyons along the rim of the Pacific Ocean basin. According to Hess, the Atlantic Ocean was expanding while the Pacific Ocean was shrinking. As old oceanic crust is consumed in the trenches, new magma rises and erupts along the spreading ridges to form new crust. In effect, the ocean basins are perpetually being 'recycled', with the creation of new crust and the destruction of old oceanic lithosphere occurring simultaneously. Thus, Hess' ideas neatly explained why the Earth does not get bigger with sea floor spreading, why there is so little sediment accumulation on the ocean floor, and why oceanic rocks are much younger than continental rocks.

Mapping with Earthquakes

During the 20th century, improvements in and greater use of seismic instruments such as seismographs enabled scientists to learn that earthquakes tend to be concentrated in specific areas, most notably along the oceanic trenches and spreading ridges. By the late 1920s, seismologists were beginning to identify several prominent earthquake zones parallel to the trenches that typically were inclined 40–60° from the horizontal and extended several hundred kilometres into the Earth. These zones later became known as Wadati-Benioff zones, or simply Benioff zones, in honor of the seismologists who first recognized them, Kiyoo Wadati of Japan and Hugo Benioff of the United States. The study of global seismicity greatly advanced in the 1960s with the establishment of the Worldwide Standardized Seismograph Network (WWSSN) to monitor the compliance of the 1963 treaty banning above-ground testing of nuclear weapons. The much-improved data from the WWSSN instruments allowed seismologists to map precisely the zones of earthquake concentration world wide.

19 Volcano

A volcano is an opening, or rupture, in a planet's surface or crust, which allows hot magma, ash and gases to escape from below the surface. The word *volcano* is derived from the name of Vulcano island off Sicily which in turn, was named after Vulcan, the Roman god of fire.

Volcanoes are generally found where tectonic plates are diverging or converging. A mid-oceanic ridge, for example the Mid-Atlantic Ridge, has examples of volcanoes caused by divergent tectonic plates pulling apart; the Pacific Ring of Fire has examples of volcanoes caused by convergent tectonic plates coming together. By contrast, volcanoes are usually not created where two tectonic plates slide past one another. Volcanoes can also form where there is stretching and thinning of the Earth's crust (called 'non-hotspot intraplate volcanism'), such as in the African Rift Valley, the Wells Gray-Clearwater volcanic field and the Rio Grande Rift in North America and the European Rhine Graben with its Eifel volcanoes.

Volcanoes can be caused by mantle plumes. These so-called hotspots, for example at Hawaii, can occur far from plate boundaries. Hotspot volcanoes are also found elsewhere in the solar system, especially on rocky planets and moons.

Divergent Plate Boundaries

At the mid-oceanic ridges, two tectonic plates diverge from one another. New oceanic crust is being formed by hot molten rock slowly cooling and solidifying. The crust is very thin at mid-oceanic ridges due to the pull of the tectonic plates. The release of pressure due to the thinning of the crust leads to adiabatic expansion, and the partial melting of the mantle causing volcanism and creating new oceanic crust. Most divergent plate boundaries are at the bottom of the oceans, therefore most volcanic activity is submarine, forming new seafloor. Black smokers or deep sea vents are an example of this kind of volcanic activity. Where the mid-oceanic ridge is above sea-level, volcanic islands are formed, for example, Iceland.

Convergent Plate Boundaries

Subduction zones are places where two plates, usually an oceanic plate and a continental plate, collide. In this case, the oceanic plate subducts, or submerges under the continental plate forming a deep ocean trench just offshore. Water released from the subducting plate lowers the melting temperature of the overlying mantle wedge, creating magma. This magma tends to be very viscous due to its high silica content, so often does not reach the surface and cools at depth. When it does reach the surface, a volcano is formed. Typical examples for this kind of volcano are Mount Etna and the volcanoes in the Pacific Ring of Fire.

Hotspots

Hotspots are not usually located on the ridges of tectonic plates, but above mantle plumes, where the convection of the Earth's mantle creates a column of hot material that rises until it reaches the crust, which tends to be thinner than in other areas of the Earth. The temperature of the plume causes the crust to melt and form pipes, which can vent magma. Because the tectonic plates move whereas the mantle plume remains in the same place, each volcano becomes dormant after a while and a new volcano is then formed as the plate shifts over the hotspot. The Hawaiian Islands are thought to be formed in such a manner, as well as the Snake River Plain, with the Yellowstone Caldera being the part of the North American plate currently above the hot spot.

Volcanic Features

The most common perception of a volcano is of a conical mountain, spewing lava and poisonous gases from a crater at its summit. This describes just one of many types of volcano, and the features of volcanoes are much more complicated. The structure and behaviour of volcanoes depends on a number of factors. Some volcanoes have rugged peaks formed by lava domes rather than a summit crater, whereas others present landscape features such as massive plateaus. Vents that issue volcanic material (lava, which is what magma is called once it has escaped to the surface, and ash) and gases (mainly steam and magmatic gases) can be located anywhere on the landform. Many of these vents give rise to smaller cones such as Pu?u ?O?o on a flank of Hawaii's.

Other types of volcano include cryovolcanoes (or ice volcanoes), particularly on some moons of Jupiter, Saturn and Neptune; and mud volcanoes, which are formations often not associated with known magmatic activity. Active mud volcanoes tend to involve temperatures much lower than those of igneous volcanoes, except when a mud volcano is actually a vent of an igneous volcano.

Shield Volcanoes

Shield volcanoes, so named for their broad, shield-like profiles, are formed by the eruption of low-viscosity lava that can flow a great distance from a vent, but not generally explode catastrophically. Since low-viscosity magma is typically low in silica, shield volcanoes are more common in oceanic than continental settings. The Hawaiian volcanic chain is a series of shield cones, and they are common in Iceland, as well.

Lava Domes

Lava domes are built by slow eruptions of highly viscous lavas. They are sometimes formed within the crater of a previous volcanic eruption (as in Mount Saint Helens), but can also form independently, as in the case of Lassen Peak. Like stratovolcanoes, they can produce violent, explosive eruptions, but their lavas generally do not flow far from the originating vent.

Cryptodomes

Cryptodomes are formed when viscous lava forces its way up and causes a bulge. The 1980 eruption of Mount St. Helens was an example. Lava was under great pressure and forced a bulge in the mountain, which was unstable and slid down the North side.

Volcanic Cones (Cinder Cones)

Volcanic cones or cinder cones are the result from eruptions that erupt mostly small pieces of scoria and pyroclastics (both resemble cinders, hence the name of this volcano type) that build up around the vent. These can be relatively short-lived eruptions that produce a cone-shaped hill perhaps 30 to 400 meters high. Most cinder cones erupt only once. Cinder cones may form as flank vents on larger volcanoes, or occur on their own. Parícutin in Mexico and Sunset Crater in Arizona are examples of cinder cones. In New Mexico, Caja del Rio is a volcanic field of over 60 cinder cones.

Stratovolcanoes (Composite Volcanoes)

Stratovolcanoes or composite volcanoes are tall conical mountains composed of lava flows and other ejecta in alternate layers, the strata that give rise to the name.

Stratovolcanoes are also known as composite volcanoes, created from several structures during different kinds of eruptions. Strato/composite volcanoes are made of cinders, ash and lava. Cinders and ash pile on top of each other, lava flows on top of the ash, where it cools and hardens, and then the process begins again. Classic examples include Mt. Fuji in Japan, Mayon Volcano in the Philippines, and Mount Vesuvius and Stromboli in Italy. In recorded history, explosive eruptions by stratovolcanoes have posed the greatest hazard to civilizations.

Supervolcanoes

A supervolcano is a large volcano that usually has a large caldera and can potentially produce devastation on an enormous, sometimes continental, scale. Such eruptions would be able to cause severe cooling of global temperatures for many years afterwards because of the huge volumes of sulfur and ash erupted. They are the most dangerous type of volcano. Examples include Yellowstone Caldera in Yellowstone National Park and Valles Caldera in New Mexico (both western United States), Lake Taupo in New Zealand, Lake Toba in Sumatra, Indonesia and Ngorogoro Crater in Tanzania. Supervolcanoes are hard to identify centuries later, given the enormous areas they cover. Large igneous provinces are also considered supervolcanoes because of the vast amount of basalt lava erupted, but are non-explosive.

Submarine Volcanoes

Submarine volcanoes are common features on the ocean floor. Some are active and, in shallow water, disclose their presence by blasting steam and rocky debris high above the surface of the sea. Many others lie at such great depths that the tremendous weight of the water above them prevents the explosive release of steam and gases, although they can be detected by hydrophones and discolouration of water because of volcanic gases. Pumice rafts may also appear. Even large submarine eruptions may not disturb the ocean surface. Because of the rapid cooling effect of water as compared to air, and increased buoyancy, submarine volcanoes often form rather steep pillars over their volcanic vents as compared to above-surface volcanoes. They may become so large that they break the ocean surface as new islands. Pillow lava is a common eruptive product of submarine volcanoes. Hydrothermal vents are common near these volcanoes, and some support peculiar ecosystems based on dissolved minerals.

Subglacial Volcanoes

Subglacial volcanoes develop underneath icecaps. They are made up of flat lava which flows at the top of extensive pillow lavas and palagonite. When the icecap melts, the lavas on the top collapse, leaving a flat-topped mountain. Then, the pillow lavas also collapse, giving an angle of 37.5 degrees. These volcanoes are also called table mountains, tuyas or (uncommonly) mobergs. Very good examples of this type of volcano can be seen in Iceland, however, there are also tuyas in British Columbia. The origin of the term comes from Tuya Butte, which is one of the several tuyas in the area of the Tuya River and Tuya Range in northern British Columbia. Tuya Butte was the first such landform analyzed and so its name has entered the geological literature for this kind of volcanic formation. The Tuya Mountains Provincial Park was recently established to protect this unusual landscape, which lies north of Tuya Lake and south of the Jennings River near the boundary with the Yukon Territory.

Mud Volcanoes

Mud volcanoes or mud domes are formations created by geo-excreted liquids and gases, although there are several different processes which may cause such activity. The largest structures are 10 kilometers in diameter and reach 700 meters high.

Lava Composition

Another way of classifying volcanoes is by the *composition of material erupted* (lava), since this affects the shape of the volcano. Lava can be broadly classified into four different compositions:

If the erupted magma contains a high percentage (>63%) of silica, the lava is called 'felsic'.

Felsic lavas (dacites or rhyolites) tend to be highly viscous (not very fluid) and are erupted as domes or short, stubby flows. Viscous lavas tend to form stratovolcanoes or lava domes. Lassen Peak in California is an example of a volcano formed from felsic lava and is actually a large lava dome.

Because siliceous magmas are so viscous, they tend to trap volatiles (gases) that are present, which cause the magma to erupt catastrophically, eventually forming stratovolcanoes. Pyroclastic flows (ignimbrites) are highly hazardous products of such volcanoes, since they are composed of molten volcanic ash too heavy to go up into the atmosphere, so they hug the volcano's slopes and travel far from their vents during large eruptions. Temperatures as high as 1,200 °C are known to occur in pyroclastic flows, which will incinerate everything flammable in their path and thick layers of hot pyroclastic flow deposits can be laid down, often up to many metres thick. Alaska's Valley of Ten Thousand Smokes, formed by the eruption of Novarupta near Katmai in 1912, is an example of a thick pyroclastic flow or ignimbrite deposit. Volcanic ash that is light enough to be erupted high into the Earth's atmosphere may travel many kilometres before it falls back to ground as a tuff.

If the erupted magma contains 52-63 per cent silica, the lava is of intermediate composition.

These 'andesitic' volcanoes generally only occur above subduction zones (*e.g.* Mount Merapi in Indonesia).

Andesitic lava is typically formed at convergent boundary margins of tectonic plates, by several processes.

Hydration melting of peridotite and fractional crystallization.

Melting of subducted slab containing sediments.

Magma mixing between felsic rhyolitic and mafic basaltic magmas in an intermediate reservoir prior to emplacement or lava flow.

If the erupted magma contains <52 per cent and >45 per cent silica, the lava is called mafic (because it contains higher percentages of magnesium (Mg) and iron (Fe)) or basaltic. These lavas are usually much less viscous than rhyolitic lavas, depending on their eruption temperature; they also tend to be hotter than felsic lavas. Mafic lavas occur in a wide range of settings.

At mid-ocean ridges, where two oceanic plates are pulling apart, basaltic lava erupts as pillows to fill the gap.

Shield volcanoes (*e.g.* the Hawaiian Islands, including Mauna Loa and Kilauea), on both oceanic and continental crust.

As continental flood basalts.

Some erupted magmas contain <=45 per cent silica and produce ultramafic lava. Ultramafic flows, also known as komatiites, are very rare; indeed, very few have been erupted at the Earth's surface since the Proterozoic, when the planet's heat flow was higher. They are (or were) the hottest lavas, and probably more fluid than common mafic lavas.

Lava Texture

Two types of lava are named according to the surface texture: (pronounced and pahoehoe , both words having Hawaiian origins. It is characterized by a rough, clinkery surface and is the typical texture of viscous lava flows. However, even basaltic or mafic flows can be erupted as flows, particularly if the eruption rate is high and the slope is steep.

Pahoehoe is characterized by its smooth and often ropey or wrinkly surface and is generally formed from more fluid lava flows. Usually, only mafic flows will erupt as pahoehoe, since they often erupt at higher temperatures or have the proper chemical make-up to allow them to flow with greater fluidity. Volcanic activity

Scientific Classification of Volcanoes

Philippine Institute of Volcanology and Seismology provides a scientific classification system for volcanoes.

- **Active**: Eruption in historic times — Historical record — 500 years — C14 dating — 10,000 years — Local seismic activity — Oral/folkloric history.
- **Potentially Active**: Solfataras/Fumaroles — Geologically young (possibly erupted < 10,000 years and for calderas and large systems — possibly < 25,000 years). Young-looking geomorphology (thin soil cover/ sparse vegetation; low degree of erosion and dissection; young vent featuresl; +/- vegetation cover). Suspected seismic activity. Documented local ground deformation — Geochemical indicators of magmatic involvement. Geophysical proof of magma bodies. Strong connection with subduction zones and external tectonic settings.
- **Inactive**: No record of eruption and its form is beginning to change by the agents of weathering and erosion via formation of deep and long gullies.

Popular Classification of Volcanoes as given below:

Active

A popular way of classifying magmatic volcanoes is by their frequency of eruption, with those that erupt regularly called active, those that have erupted in historical times but are now quiet called dormant, and those that have not erupted in historical times called extinct. However, these popular classifications — extinct in particular — are practically meaningless to scientists. They use classifications which refer to a particular volcano's formative and eruptive processes and resulting shapes, which was explained above.

There is no real consensus among volcanologists on how to define an 'active' volcano. The lifespan of a volcano can vary from months to several million years, making such a distinction sometimes meaningless when compared to the lifespans of humans or even civilizations. For example, many of Earth's volcanoes have erupted dozens of times in the past few thousand years but are not currently showing signs of eruption. Given the long lifespan of such volcanoes, they are very active. By human lifespans, however, they are not.

Scientists usually consider a volcano to be erupting or likely to erupt if it is currently erupting, or showing signs of unrest such as unusual earthquake activity or significant new gas emissions. Most scientists consider a volcano *active* if it has erupted in holocene times. Historic times is another timeframe for *active*. But it is important to note that the span of recorded history differs from region to region. In China and the Mediterranean, recorded history reaches back more than 3,000 years but in the Pacific Northwest of the United States and Canada, it reaches back less than 300 years, and in Hawaii and New Zealand, only around 200 years. The Smithsonian Global Volcanism Programme's definition of *active* is having erupted within the last 10,000 years (the 'holocene' period).

Extinct

Extinct volcanoes are those that scientists consider unlikely to erupt again, because the volcano no longer has a lava supply. Examples of extinct volcanoes are many volcanoes on the Hawaiian Islands in the U.S. (extinct because the Hawaii hotspot is centered near the Big Island), and Paricutin, which is monogenetic. Otherwise, whether a volcano is truly extinct is often difficult to determine. Since 'supervolcano' calderas can have eruptive lifespans sometimes measured in millions of years, a caldera that has not produced an eruption in tens of thousands of years is likely to be considered dormant instead of extinct. For example, the Yellowstone Caldera in Yellowstone National Park is at least 2 million years old and hasn't erupted violently for approximately 6,40,000 years, although there has been some minor activity relatively recently, with hydrothermal eruptions less than 10,000 years ago and lava flows about 70,000 years ago. For this reason, scientists do not consider the Yellowstone Caldera extinct. In fact, because the caldera has frequent earthquakes, a very active geothermal system (*i.e.* the entirety of the geothermal activity found in Yellowstone National Park), and rapid rates of ground uplift, many scientists consider it to be an active volcano.

There are many different types of volcanic eruptions and associated activity: phreatic eruptions (steam-generated eruptions), explosive eruption of high-silica lava (*e.g.*, rhyolite), effusive eruption of low-silica lava (*e.g.*, basalt), pyroclastic flows, lahars (debris flow) and carbon dioxide emission. All of these activities can pose a hazard to humans. Earthquakes, hot springs, fumaroles, mud pots and geysers often accompany volcanic activity.

The concentrations of different volcanic gases can vary considerably from one volcano to the next. Water vapour is typically the most abundant volcanic gas, followed by carbon dioxide and sulfur dioxide. Other principal volcanic gases include hydrogen sulfide, hydrogen chloride, and hydrogen fluoride. A large number of minor and trace gases are also found in volcanic emissions, for example hydrogen, carbon monoxide, halocarbons, organic compounds, and volatile metal chlorides.

Large, explosive volcanic eruptions inject water vapour (H_2O), carbon dioxide (CO_2), sulfur dioxide (SO_2), hydrogen chloride (HCl), hydrogen fluoride (HF) and ash (pulverized rock and pumice) into the stratosphere to heights of 16-32 kilometres (10-20 miles) above the Earth's surface. The most significant impacts from these injections come from the conversion of sulfur dioxide to sulfuric acid (H_2SO_4), which condenses rapidly in the stratosphere to form fine sulfate aerosols. The aerosols increase the Earth's albedo — its reflection of radiation from the Sun back into space — and thus cool the Earth's lower atmosphere or troposphere; however, they also absorb heat radiated up from the Earth, thereby warming the stratosphere. Several eruptions during the past century have caused a decline in the average temperature at the Earth's surface of up to half a degree (Fahrenheit scale) for periods of one to three years — sulfur dioxide from the eruption of Huaynaputina probably caused the Russian famine of 1601-1603. The sulfate aerosols also promote complex chemical reactions on their surfaces that alter chlorine and nitrogen chemical species in the stratosphere. This effect, together with increased stratospheric chlorine levels from chlorofluorocarbon pollution, generates chlorine monoxide (ClO), which destroys ozone (O_3). As the aerosols grow and coagulate, they settle down into the upper troposphere where they serve as nuclei for cirrus clouds and further modify the Earth's radiation balance. Most of the hydrogen chloride (HCl) and hydrogen fluoride (HF) are dissolved in water droplets in the eruption cloud and quickly fall to the ground as acid rain. The injected ash also falls rapidly from the stratosphere; most of it is removed within several days to a few weeks. Finally, explosive volcanic eruptions release the greenhouse gas carbon dioxide and thus provide a deep source of carbon for biogeochemical cycles.

Gas emissions from volcanoes are a natural contributor to acid rain. Volcanic activity releases about 130 to 230 teragrams (145 million to 255 million short tons) of carbon dioxide each year. Volcanic eruptions may inject aerosols into the Earth's atmosphere. Large injections may cause visual effects such as unusually colourful sunsets and affect global climate mainly by cooling it. Volcanic eruptions also provide the benefit of adding nutrients to soil through the weathering process of volcanic rocks. These fertile soils assist the growth of plants and various crops. Volcanic eruptions can also create new islands, as the magma cools and solidifies upon contact with the water.

Magma

Magma is molten rock that is found beneath the surface of the Earth, and may also exist on other terrestrial planets. Besides molten rock, magma may also contain suspended crystals and gas bubbles. Magma often collects in a magma chamber inside a volcano. Magma is capable of intrusion into adjacent rocks, extrusion onto the surface as lava, and explosive ejection as tephra to form pyroclastic rock.

Magma is a complex high-temperature fluid substance. Temperatures of most magmas are in the range 700 °C to 1300 °C (or 1300 °F to 2400 °F), but very rare carbonatite melts may be as cool as 600 °C, and komatiite melts may have been as hot as 1600 °C. Most are silicate solutions.

Environments of magma formation and compositions are commonly correlated. Environments include subduction zones, continental rift zones, mid-oceanic ridges, and hotspots, some of which are interpreted as mantle plumes. Despite being found in such widespread locales, the bulk of the Earth's crust and mantle is not molten. Rather, most of the Earth takes the form of a rheid, a form of solid that can move or deform under pressure. Magma, as liquid, preferentially forms in high temperature, low pressure environments within several kilometers of the Earth's surface.

Magma compositions may evolve after formation by fractional crystallization, contamination, and magma mixing. By definition, all igneous rock is formed from magma.

While the study of magma has historically relied on observing magma in the form of lava outflows, magma has been encountered in situ three times during drilling projects — twice in Iceland, and once in Hawaii.

Melting of Solid Rock

Melting of solid rock to form magma is controlled by three physical parameters: its temperature, pressure, and composition. Mechanisms are discussed in the entry for igneous rock.

Temperature

At any given pressure and for any given composition of rock, a rise in temperature past the solidus will cause melting. Within the solid earth, the temperature of a rock is controlled by the geothermal gradient and the radioactive decay within the rock. The geothermal gradient averages about 25 °C/km with a wide range from a low of 5-10 °C/km within oceanic trenches and subduction zones to 30-80 °C/km under mid-ocean ridges and volcanic arc environments.

Pressure

As magma buoyantly rises it will cross the solidus-liquidus and its temperature will reduce by adiabatic cooling. At this point it will liquefy and if erupted onto the surface will form lava. Melting can also occur due to a reduction in pressure by a process known as decompression melting.

Composition

It is usually very difficult to change the bulk composition of a large mass of rock, so composition is the basic control on whether a rock will melt at any given temperature and pressure. The composition of a rock may also be considered to include volatile phases such as water and carbon dioxide.

The presence of volatile phases in a rock under pressure can stabilize a melt fraction. The presence of even 0.8 per cent water may reduce the temperature of melting by as much as 100 °C. Conversely, the loss of water and volatiles from a magma may cause it to essentially freeze or solidify.

Also a major portion of all magma is silica, which is a compound of silicon and oxygen. Magma also contains gases, which expand as the magma rises. Magma that is high in silica resists flowing, so expanding gases are trapped in it. Pressure builds up until the gases blast out in a violent, dangerous explosion. Magma that is relatively poor in silica flows easily, so gas bubbles move up through it and escape fairly gently. Though an eruption of silica-poor magma can throw lava high into the air, forming lava fountains, visitors can usually watch safely nearby.

Magma rises toward Earth's surface as long as it is less dense than the surrounding rock. Once magma stops rising, it can collect in areas called magma chambers. Magma can remain in a chamber until it cools, forming igneous rock, or it can erupt. Volcanic eruptions occur when, for example, a chamber is not large enough to hold additional magma that pushes in. When magma erupts, it is called lava.

Partial Melting

When rocks melt they do so incrementally and gradually; most rocks are made of several minerals, all of which have different melting points, and the phase diagrams that control melting are often complex. As a rock melts, its volume changes. When enough rock is melted, the small globules of melt (generally occurring in between mineral grains) link up and soften the rock. Under pressure within the earth, as little as a fraction of a per cent partial melting may be sufficient to cause melt to be squeezed from its source.

Melts can stay in place long enough to melt to 20 per cent or even 35 per cent, but rocks are rarely melted in excess of 50 per cent, because eventually the melted rock mass becomes a crystal and melt mush that can then ascend *en masse* as a diapir, which may then cause further decompression melting.

Primary Melts

When a rock melts, the liquid is known as a primary melt. Primary melts have not undergone any differentiation and represent the starting composition of a magma. In nature it is rare to find primary melts. The leucosomes of migmatites are examples of primary melts. Primary melts derived from the mantle are especially important, and are known as primitive melts or primitive magmas. By finding the primitive magma composition of a magma series it is possible to model the composition of the mantle from which a melt was formed, which is important in understanding evolution of the mantle.

Geochemical Implications of Partial Melting

The degree of partial melting is critical for determining what type of magma is produced. The degree of partial melting required to form a melt can be estimated by considering the relative enrichment of incompatible elements versus compatible elements. Incompatible elements commonly include potassium, barium, caesium, rubidium.

Rock types produced by small degrees of partial melting in the Earth's mantle are typically alkaline (Ca, Na), potassic (K) and/or peralkaline (high aluminium to silica ratio). Typically, primitive melts of this composition form lamprophyre, lamproite, kimberlite and sometimes nepheline-bearing mafic rocks such as alkali basalts and essexite gabbros or even carbonatite.

Pegmatite may be produced by low degrees of partial melting of the crust. Some granite-composition magmas are eutectic (or cotectic) melts, and they may be produced by low to high degrees of partial melting of the crust, as well as by fractional crystallization. At high degrees of partial melting of the crust, granitoids such as tonalite, granodiorite and monzonite can be produced, but other mechanisms are typically important in producing them.

At high degrees of partial melting of the mantle, komatiite and picrite are produced.

Composition and Melt Structure and Properties

Silicate melts are composed mainly of silicon, oxygen, aluminium, alkalis (sodium, potassium, calcium), magnesium and iron. Silicon atoms are in tetrahedral coordination with oxygen, as in almost all silicate minerals, but in melts atomic order is preserved only over short distances. The physical behaviours of melts depend upon their atomic structures as well as upon temperature and pressure and composition.

Viscosity is a key melt property in understanding the behaviour of magmas. More silica-rich melts are typically more polymerized, with more linkage of silica tetrahedra, and so are more viscous. Dissolution of water drastically reduces melt viscosity. Higher-temperature melts are less viscous.

Generally speaking, more mafic magmas, such as those that form basalt, are hotter and less viscous than more silica-rich magmas, such as those that form rhyolite. Low viscosity leads to gentler, less explosive eruptions.

Parental Melts

Where it is impossible to find the primitive or primary magma composition, it is often useful to attempt to identify a parental melt. A parental melt is a magma composition from which the observed range of magma chemistries has been derived by the processes of igneous differentiation. It need not be a primitive melt.

For instance, a series of basalt flows are assumed to be related to one another. A composition from which they could reasonably be produced by fractional crystallization is termed a parental melt. Fractional crystallization models would be produced to test the hypothesis that they share a common parental melt.

Dust

Dust is a general name for minute solid particles with diameters less than 20 thou (500 micrometres). Particles in the atmosphere arise from various sources such as soil dust lifted up by wind, volcanic eruptions, and pollution. Dust in homes, offices, and other human environments contains human skin cells, small amounts of plant pollen, human and animal hairs, textile fibers, paper fibres, minerals from outdoor soil, and many other materials which may be found in the local environment.

Domestic Dust: Composition and Types

"The quantity and composition of house dust varies greatly with seasonal and environmental factors such as the surroundings, exchange of outside air, age of the house, building materials and their condition, and the quantity of furniture and carpets, as well as their state of preservation. The composition of dust also depends upon the ventilation, and heating systems, cleaning habits, activities of the occupants or users of a room, etc. House dust consists of inorganic and organic matter, and the relative proportions of these components may vary considerably. Kindergartens dust often consists almost entirely of inorganic materials like sand, loam, and clay from sand pits. On the other hand, house dust from the homes of animal owners with worn out carpets consists nearly completely of organic material. In a study of 318 house samples, the proportion of organic matter ranged from between <5 per cent and >95 per cent. Fergusson, et al. reported the organic content of house dust from 11 homes in Christchurch, New Zealand, ranged from 25.7 per cent to 56.5 per cent. Floor dust from seven Danish offices had a mean organic fraction of 33 per cent (Mølhave et al., 2000)".

According to the *German Environmental Survey*, approximately 6 mg/(m^2·d) of house dust is formed in private households depending primarily on the amount of time spent at home. Nearly 1000 dust particles per square centimetre settle on domestic surfaces every hour. Some dust consists of human skin. Scientists estimate that humans shed the entire outer layer of skin every day or two, at a rate of 7 million skin flakes per minute, which corresponds to a mass emission rate of about 20 milligrams per minute. "Dust bunnies" are small clumps of fluff that form when sufficient dust accumulates.

Dust particles acquire a negative charge when introduced into a low pressure RF argon plasma and levitate in the sheath of the lower RF driven electrode due to a balance between the upward electrostatic force and the downward forces of ion drag and gravity. An external negative DC voltage greater than the negative self-bias is applied to the driven electrode, which further repels the plasma electrons so increasing the sheath size and moving the equilibrium height of the dust particles upwards. Increasing the negative DC voltage is found to cause the lowest dust particles to fall through the sheath to the driven electrode. The trajectories of these falling particles have been recorded with a high speed camera and analysed. The charge on the dust particles is deduced from the equation of motion. It is found that the dust particles always remain negatively charged even deep in the sheath.

Domestic Dust and Humans

Insects and other small fauna found in houses subtly interact with dust and may have adverse impact on the health of humans.

Dust may worsen hay fever. Circulating outdoor air through a house by keeping doors and windows open, or at least slightly ajar, may reduce the risk of hay fever-causing dust. In colder climates, occupants seal even the smallest air gaps, and eliminate outside fresh air circulating inside the house. So it is essential to manage dust and airflow.

House dust mites exist on all indoor surfaces and even suspended in the air. They feed on minute particles of organic matter, the main constituent of house dust. Dust mites flourish in the fibers of bedding, furniture, and carpets. They excrete enzymes to digest the organic particles, and excrete feces, that together become part of the house dust, and may irritate allergies.

Alternately, the hygiene hypothesis posits that the modern obsession with cleanliness is as much a problem as house dust mites. The hygiene hypothesis argues that our lack of prior pathogenic exposure may in fact *encourage* the development of ailments including hay fever and asthma.

Atmospheric Dust

Airborne dust is considered an aerosol and can have a strong local radiative forcing on the atmosphere and significant effects on climate. In addition, if enough minute particles are dispersed within the air in a given area (such as flour or coal dust), under certain circumstances can cause an explosion hazard.

Coal dust is responsible for the lung disease known as Pneumoconiosis, including black lung disease, that occurs among coal miners. The danger of coal dust resulted in environmental legislation regulating work place air quality in some jurisdictions.

Road Dust

Dust kicked up by vehicles travelling on roads, may make up 33 per cent of air pollution. Road dust consists of deposition of vehicle exhausts and industrial exhausts, tire and brake wears, dust from paved roads or potholes, and dust from construction sites. Road dust represents a significant source contributing to the generation and release of particulate matter into the atmosphere. Control of road dust is a significant challenge in urban areas, and also in other spheres with high levels of vehicular traffic upon unsealed roads such as mines and garbage dumps. Road dust may be suppressed by mechanical methods like sweeping vehicles, with vegetable oils, or with water sprayers.

Dust Control

Dust control is the suppression of solid particles with diameters less than 500 micrometers. Dust in the airstream poses a serious health threat to children, older people, and those with respiratory illnesses.

Control of Domestic Dust

House dust can become airborne easily. Care should be exercised when removing dust to avoid causing the dust to become airborne. Some dust removing devices trap some dust, but broadcast some dust into the air, which may settle in the cleaner's lungs, and make the activity hazardous . One way to repel dust is with an electrical charge Water-trap vacuums such as the Rainbow, eliminate the risk of broadcasting dust by drowning the dust particles in water. Dust subsequently cannot escape the container to fly back into the air.

Control of Atmospheric Dust

The U.S. Environmental Protection Agency (EPA) mandates facilities that generate dust minimize or mitigate the production of dust in their operation. The most frequent dust control violations occur at new residential housing developments in urban areas. United States Federal law requires that construction sites obtain permits to conduct earth moving, and include plans to control dust emissions. Control measures include such simple practices as spraying construction and demolition sites with water, and preventing the tracking of dust onto adjacent roads. US federal laws require dust control on sources such as vacant lots, unpaved parking lots, and unpaved roads. Dust in such places may be suppressed by mechanical methods, including paving or laying down gravel, or stabilizing the surface with water, vegetable oils or other dust suppressants, or by using water misters to suppress dust that is already airborne.

Dust in Outer Space

Cosmic dust is widely present in space, where gas and dust clouds are primary precursors for planetary systems. The zodiacal light seen in the dark night sky, is produced by sunlight reflected from particles of dust in orbit around the Sun. The tails of comets are produced by emissions of dust and ionized gas from the body of the comet. Dust also covers solid planetary bodies, and vast dust storms occur on Mars that cover almost the entire planet. Interstellar dust is found between the stars, and high concentrations produce diffuse nebulae and reflection nebulae.

Dust is widely present in the galaxy. Ambient radiation heats dust and re-emits radiation into the microwave band, which may distort the cosmic microwave background power spectrum. Dust in this regime has a complicated emission spectrum, and includes both thermal dust emission and spinning dust emission.

Dust samples returned from outer space may provide information about conditions in the early solar system. Several spacecraft have sought to gather samples of dust and other materials. Among these craft was Stardust, which flew past Comet Wild 2 in 2004, and returned a capsule of the comet's remains to Earth in January 2006. The Japanese Hayabusa spacecraft is on a mission to collect samples of dust from the surface of an asteroid.

Index

E

F

G

H

I